Activity Book

Science

Editorial Offices: Glenview, Illinois • Parsippany, New Jersey • New York, New York
Sales Offices: Needham, Massachusetts • Duluth, Georgia • Glenview, Illinois
Coppell, Texas • Sacramento, California • Mesa, Arizona

PEARSON
Scott
Foresman

www.sfsuccessnet.com

Series Authors

Dr. Timothy Cooney
*Professor of Earth Science and
Science Education*
University of Northern Iowa (UNI)
Cedar Falls, Iowa

Dr. Jim Cummins
Professor
Department of Curriculum,
Teaching, and Learning
The University of Toronto
Toronto, Canada

Dr. James Flood
*Distinguished Professor of Literacy
and Language*
School of Teacher Education
San Diego State University
San Diego, California

Barbara Kay Foots, M.Ed.
Science Education Consultant
Houston, Texas

Dr. M. Jenice Goldston
*Associate Professor of Science
Education*
Department of Elementary Education
Programs
University of Alabama
Tuscaloosa, Alabama

Dr. Shirley Gholston Key
*Associate Professor of Science
Education*
Instruction and Curriculum Leadership
Department
College of Education
University of Memphis
Memphis, Tennessee

Dr. Diane Lapp
*Distinguished Professor of Reading
and Language Arts in Teacher
Education*
San Diego State University
San Diego, California

Sheryl A. Mercier
Classroom Teacher
Dunlap Elementary School
Dunlap, California

Dr. Karen Ostlund
UTeach, College of Natural Sciences
The University of Texas at Austin
Austin, Texas

Dr. Nancy Romance
*Professor of Science Education
& Principal Investigator*
NSF/IERI Science IDEAS Project
Charles E. Schmidt College
of Science
Florida Atlantic University
Boca Raton, Florida

Dr. William Tate
*Chair and Professor of Education
and Applied Statistics*
Department of Education
Washington University
St. Louis, Missouri

Dr. Kathryn C. Thornton
Professor
School of Engineering and
Applied Science
University of Virginia
Charlottesville, Virginia

Dr. Leon Ukens
Professor of Science Education
Department of Physics, Astronomy,
and Geosciences
Towson University
Towson, Maryland

Steve Weinberg
Consultant
Connecticut Center for
Advanced Technology
East Hartford, Connecticut

Consulting Author

Dr. Michael P. Klentschy
Superintendent
El Centro Elementary School District
El Centro, California

ISBN: 0-328-12626-8

Unit A
Life Science

Unit B
Earth Science

Unit C
Physical Science

Unit D
Space and Technology

Science Safety

Scientists know they must work safely when doing experiments. You need to be careful when doing science activities too. Follow these safety rules.

- Read the activity carefully before you start to do it.
- Listen to the teacher's instructions. Ask questions about things you do not understand.
- Wear safety goggles when needed.
- Keep your work place neat and clean. Clean up spills right away.
- Never taste or smell substances unless directed to do so by your teacher.
- Handle sharp items and other equipment carefully.
- Use chemicals carefully.
- Help keep plants and animals you use safe.
- Tell your teacher if you have an accident or you see something that looks unsafe.
- Put materials away when you finish an inquiry.
- Dispose of chemicals properly.
- Wash your hands well when you are finished.

Practice Observing

Observe means to gather information using one or more of the five senses: sight, sound, touch, taste, or smell. Sometimes it is necessary to use equipment to make an observation. In this activity, you will observe where different objects have their center of gravity and how an object's center of gravity may be changed.

Materials

CD case/jewel box   scissors with plastic handles
metric ruler   spoon
marker   rubber eraser

What to Do

❶ Stand the CD case upright on one edge. The case is the fulcrum, or balancing point, for the activity.

❷ Balance the ruler perpendicularly across the top edge of the CD case as in the diagram below. The ruler's center of gravity is the point where it sits balanced on the case. Note the location of the center of gravity and record your observations on the data sheet.

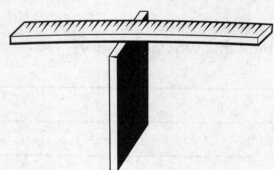

❸ Repeat step 2 with an eraser placed on one end of the ruler. Observe any change in the ruler's center of gravity and record your observations on the data sheet.

❹ Now measure the lengths of the scissors and the spoon. Divide each length in half to find that object's midpoint (center), and record the information on the data sheet. Then use the marker to mark the midpoint of each object.

❺ Repeat step 2 with the scissors and the spoon, each placed on the CD case. Mark the center of gravity of each object and record your observations.

Object	Length	Midpoint (length/2)	Center of Gravity: Observations
Ruler			
Ruler with eraser			
Scissors			
Spoon			

Explain Your Results

1. In step 3, what did you have to do to balance the ruler with the eraser on it? Why do you think this was necessary?

_____

_____

_____

_____

2. Where is the center of gravity of an object usually located? Use your observations from step 5 to explain your answer.

_____

_____

_____

_____

Practice Communicating

Communicate means to give or exchange information about what you learn, using words, pictures, charts, graphs, and diagrams. In this activity, you and your partner will communicate your sensation of cold and warmth and describe how your senses adapt to changes in temperature.

Materials

3 large cups
hot tap water
warm (room temperature) tap water

cold tap water
clock or timer
paper towels for drying

What to Do

1 Work with a partner. Fill one cup with cold water, one cup with warm water, and one cup with hot water. Make sure to test the hot water with your finger. If it is too hot, add a little cold water.

2 Put both hands in the cup of warm water. Describe the temperature of the water using words and a scale from 1 to 10 (1 is "very cold" and 10 is "very hot"). Have your partner record your results in the chart below.

	Your Observations	**Your Partner's Observations**
Step 2: Both hands in warm water.		

3 Now put one hand in the hot water and the other hand in the cold water. Rate the sensations and temperatures felt by each hand, and have your partner record the results.

4 Keep your hands in the water for two minutes, and then describe the water temperatures again. Have your partner record the results.

5 Now quickly place both hands in the cup of warm water. Describe the sensations and temperatures felt by each hand, and have your partner record the results.

6 Now it's your partner's turn to test the waters and your turn to record the descriptions and ratings on the chart.

Description and Rating (1 = very cold and 10 = very hot)

	Hot Water (left hand)	Cold Water (right hand)	Hot Water (left hand)	Cold Water (right hand)
Step 3: Initial reading				
Step 4: After 2 minutes				
Step 5: After warm water bath				

Explain Your Results

1. At which step did both of your hands come the closest to feeling the same temperature? Explain why.

_____

_____

_____

2. You can also communicate the results of this experiment using a line graph. Plot the numerical data and connect the points from your experiment on the graphs below.

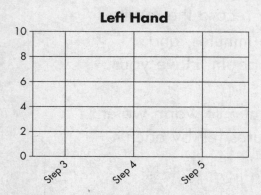

Left Hand

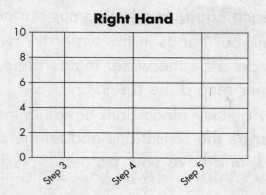

Right Hand

© Pearson Education, Inc.

Practice Estimating and Measuring

Estimate means to make a reasonable guess about a quantity, based on observations and what is already known. **Measure** means make a calculation about a quantity or size. In this activity, you will estimate and then measure the magnifying power of two lenses.

Materials

2 different magnifying glasses   small rock or other object
ruler   sheet of lined notebook paper
coin

What to Do

❶ Work with a partner and do this activity while standing. Place the coin on a table and hold the ruler upright next to it. Have your partner hold the first magnifying glass above the coin at a height of 15 cm.

❷ Take turns looking at the coin under the magnifying glass. Estimate the power of the lens by judging how many times larger the coin appears. On your data sheet, write the number of times that the coin looks magnified, followed by the symbol "x."

❸ Repeat steps 1 and 2 with the rock or other object. Make sure to keep the magnifying glass at the same height.

❹ Now carefully shade in one row on a sheet of lined notebook paper with your pencil. Look at it under the magnifying glass from the same height of 15 cm. Measure the power of the lens by counting how many lined rows outside the glass equal the single shaded row under the glass, as shown below. Then record the power of the lens in the data sheet.

❺ Repeat steps 1–4 with the second magnifying glass.

	Magnifying Glass #1		Magnifying Glass #2	
	coin	rock (second object)	coin	rock (second object)
Estimated lens power				
Measured lens power				

Explain Your Results

1. How do your two estimates of lens power for each magnifying glass compare with the measured power? Why do you think each magnifying glass was tested with two different objects?

_____

_____

_____

2. What unit of measurement was used in this activity? What other units of measurement could have been used?

_____

_____

_____

Practice Collecting Data

Collecting data means gathering information such as observations and measurements in an organized way. The information can be recorded and arranged in charts, tables, graphs, diagrams, or lists of written descriptions. In this activity, you will collect data on the mineral content of different types of water and organize the data into a bar graph.

Materials

4 empty plastic soda bottles (20 oz) with caps	tap water
measuring cup	purified water
teaspoon	spring water
ruler	Epsom salt (magnesium sulfate)
	liquid soap

What to Do

1. Remove the product labels on the soda bottles. Make sure the bottles are empty and rinsed clean.

2. Pour 250 mL (about 1 cup) of purified water into one bottle, and add 10 mL (about 2 teaspoons) of Epsom salt. Cap the bottle and swirl around until the salt dissolves.

3. Add one drop of liquid soap to the Epsom salt solution. Cap the bottle and shake it hard for five seconds.

4. Wait a few seconds for the resulting suds to form a layer of foam on top of the water. Measure the height of the foam and record it in the "Epsom" column of the data sheet chart.

5. Repeat steps 3 and 4 with the same bottle, adding one drop of liquid soap at a time to the Epsom salt solution and recording your results. Repeat until you have added a total of four drops of soap.

6. Now take a new soda bottle and repeat steps 2 through 5 with 250 mL of spring water. This time, do NOT add Epsom salt to the water.

7. Repeat step 6 using tap water and then purified water, and record your results.

Soap Foam (cm)				
	Epsom salt (magnesium sulfate) solution	**Spring water**	**Tap water**	**Purified water**
1				
2				
3				
4				

(Row labels on left: **Liquid Soap** (# of drops))

Explain Your Results

1. "Hard" water contains minerals (calcium and magnesium) that make it more difficult for soapsuds to form. Based on the data you collected, which water is the hardest? The softest? Explain your answer.

_____

_____

_____

2. Bar graphs are used to show data collected for several different items. Use your data to complete the bar graph below.

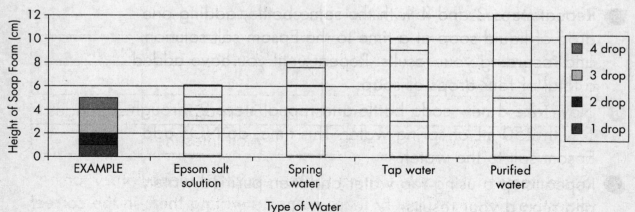

Practice Classifying

Classifying means to arrange objects, events, or living things into different groups, based on observations of their properties and a known system of order. In this activity, you will classify different parts of the body according to their body systems and functions.

Materials

pencil
diagrams of human body

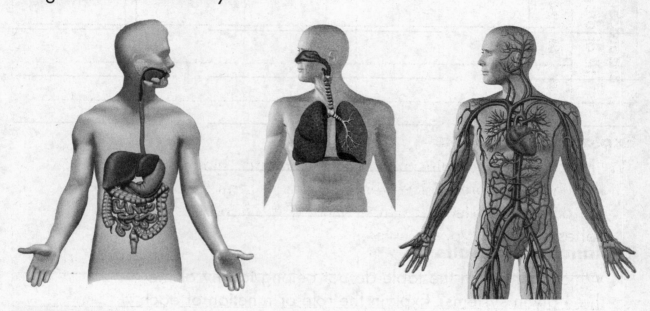

What to Do

❶ The diagrams above shows the circulatory, respiratory, and digestive systems in the human body. Use what you know about the role or function of each system and observe the different parts of the body that are included.

❷ Now look over the following table of items.

lungs	heart	bronchi	eyes	brain
blood	stomach	skull	veins	liver
pancreas	skin	large intestine	diaphragm	esophagus
ears	saliva	arteries	small intestine	nose

❸ Some items in the table belong to the respiratory, circulatory, or digestive systems. Classify these items by writing them in the correct places in the tree diagram on page 10.

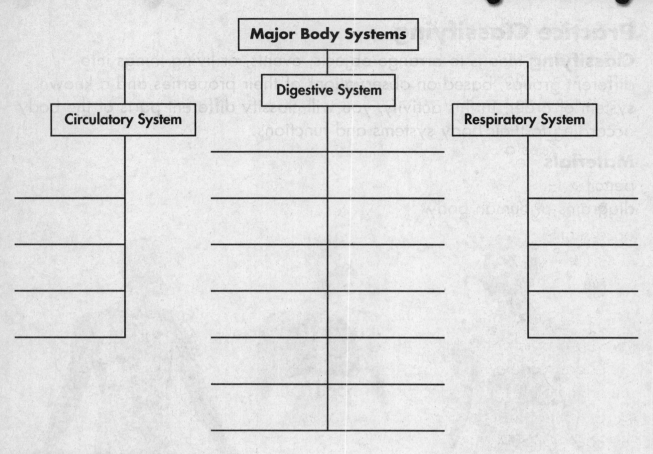

Explain Your Results

1. Which items from the table do not belong to any of the three given systems? Explain the role or function of each of these items.

_____

_____

_____

_____

_____

2. What criteria other than function could be used to classify the items in the table?

_____

_____

_____

Practice Inferring

Inferring means developing ideas and conclusions by using observations and making evaluations based on past experiences. In this activity, you will use experimental data and what you already know about erosion to determine how different types of soil interact with water.

Materials

magnifying glass	water
large funnel	sandy soil
2 measuring cups	loam (potting) soil
3 paper coffee filters	clay ("heavy") soil

What to Do

1 Rub a pinch of each type of soil between your thumb and finger to determine its texture. Write a description of how each soil feels in the chart on page 12.

2 Use the magnifying glass to look closely at a handful of each soil. Break any clumps to identify and compare the different particles in each soil. Record your observations.

3 Fill one measuring cup with 250 mL (about 1 cup) of water. Line the funnel with a coffee filter and then put a handful of sandy soil into it.

4 Hold the funnel over the second measuring cup and slowly pour the water over the sandy soil as in the diagram at right. If the funnel fills up with water, wait until the water level goes down before adding the rest. Observe what happens and measure how much water drains into the cup. Record your observations.

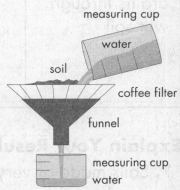

measuring cup

water

soil

coffee filter

funnel

measuring cup
water

5 Toss out the collected water and repeat step 4 using the wet soil already in the funnel. Record your observations.

6 Now repeat steps 3, 4, and 5 with the loam and clay soil. Use about the same amount of soil each time.

	Sandy soil	Loam (potting) soil	Clay (heavy) soil
Texture: How soil feels			
Soil particles: Type and size			
Steps 3 & 4: How water drains through dry soil			
Step 5: How water drains through wet soil			

Explain Your Results

1. Soils made of very small, fine particles drain water poorly and are easily carried away by winds when dry. Use your observations to infer which type of soil is being described above, and explain your answer.

_____

_____

Practice Predicting

Predicting means forming an idea of what a future result will be. Scientific predictions are made using inferences based on past experience and scientific models. In this activity, you will predict the results of an investigation on evaporation before you do it. Then you will compare the predicted and actual results.

Materials

graphing paper	water
black or blue watercolor paint	hand or dishtowel (at least 40 cm ×
paintbrush	55 cm)
five plastic cups	clock or timer

What to Do

❶ Work with a partner. Stand four plastic cups upside down on a table, and arrange them in a rectangle.

❷ Soak the towel in water and wring some of the water out. Then drape the wet towel over the cups to make a "humidity tent," as shown below.

❸ Take a sheet of graphing paper and cut it in half. Give one half to your partner and keep one for yourself. Draw a square with 10 columns and 10 rows. Fill the last plastic cup with water and use watercolors to color in your square. You and your partner should finish your paintings at the same time.

❹ Slip one painting underneath the humidity tent, and set the other painting next to it.

❺ Which painting will dry first? Write your prediction below.

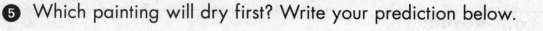

_____

_____

_____

6 Every two minutes, look at your painting and count the number of boxes that have dried in that time. Mark each dry box with an "X" so you don't count it twice. Record your data in the chart below.

7 When you are finished, copy your partner's data and compare your results.

Start time: _____	# of Dry Squares	
	Covered Painting (humidity tent)	**Uncovered Painting (table)**
2 min.		
4 min.		
6 min.		
8 min.		
10 min.		
Total:		

Explain Your Results

1. Was your prediction correct or incorrect?

_____

2. Describe what happens when paint dries, and explain why one painting dried before the other.

_____

_____

_____

3. Predict what might happen if a fan was blowing on the uncovered painting on the table. Would the paint dry faster or slower? Explain.

_____

_____

Practice Making and Using Models

Making and using models means to create simple representations or descriptions and use them to explain ideas, objects, or events. In this activity, you and your partner will model the Moon's orbit around Earth and use the model to demonstrate the different phases of the Moon.

Materials

white polystyrene foam ball (at least 5 cm)   bright flashlight
pencil   a dark room

What to Do

1 Work with a partner. Stick the end of the pencil into the polystyrene foam ball to give it a handle. Give your partner the flashlight and your Activity Book. Then sit about 1 meter apart and face each other.

2 In this model, you represent Earth and the ball is the Moon. To model the Sun and its rays, have your partner turn the flashlight on and keep it pointed at your chin throughout each of the following steps as in the diagram.

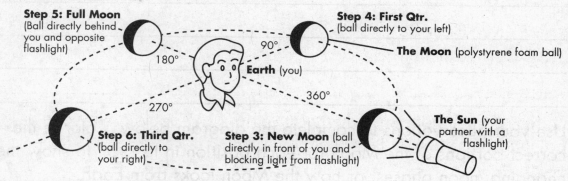

Step 5: Full Moon (Ball directly behind you and opposite flashlight)

Step 4: First Qtr. (ball directly to your left)

The Moon (polystyrene foam ball)

90°

180°

Earth (you)

360°

270°

Step 6: Third Qtr. (ball directly to your right)

Step 3: New Moon (ball directly in front of you and blocking light from flashlight)

The Sun (your partner with a flashlight)

3 New Moon: Use your left hand to hold the Moon out in front of you, so it is directly between the light from the flashlight and your eyes. Now you and your partner each describe how much of the Moon is visible from your positions. Record both your results in your chart on page 16.

4 Steps 4–6: Use the diagram to simulate first quarter, full, and third quarter Moon. Record both your results in the chart.

7 Complete the Moon's orbit by slowly bringing it back to the starting (new Moon) position. Then repeat the activity with your partner holding the Moon and you holding the Sun. This time, record all results on your partner's chart.

Different Views of the Moon

Moon Phase	Side facing Earth (Your Observations)	Side facing the Sun (Partner's Observations)
Step 3: New Moon		
Step 4: First Quarter		
Step 5: Full Moon		
Step 6: Third Quarter		

Explain Your Results

1. Compare your views of the Moon from Earth with your partner's views from the Sun's position. Explain why your views were different.

_____

_____

_____

_____

2. Use your observations to complete the diagram below. Color in the correct portions of the Moon for each position in its orbit to show the changing moon phases, or how the Moon looks from Earth.

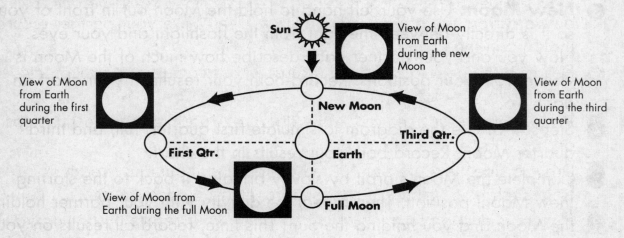

Sun

View of Moon from Earth during the new Moon

View of Moon from Earth during the first quarter

View of Moon from Earth during the third quarter

New Moon

Third Qtr.

First Qtr.

Earth

Full Moon

View of Moon from Earth during the full Moon

© Pearson Education, Inc.

Practice Interpreting Data

Interpreting data means explaining the meaning of information in tables, charts, graphs, and diagrams. You can find answers to scientific questions by interpreting the data you collect. In this activity, you will perform an experiment with water and then interpret the data in order to answer questions about water pressure.

Materials

ruler

empty cardboard juice or
  milk carton (64 oz, or 2 qt)

screwdriver

masking tape

water

baking pan

What to Do

1. Work with a partner. Use the screwdriver to punch three holes on the same side of the carton. The lowest hole should be 8 cm from the bottom of the carton. The second hole should be 13 cm from the bottom and the third should be 18 cm from the bottom.

2. Cover the three holes with a single strip of masking tape, top to bottom.

3. Fill the carton with tap water.

4. Hold the carton over the edge of the baking pan. Make sure the holes are facing the baking pan.

5. Quickly remove the tape. When all three holes are uncovered, have your partner measure the distance each stream of water travels outward from the bottom of the carton. Then have your partner record the data in the chart on page 18.

6. Describe the general shape and direction of each water stream. Have your partner record the data.

7. When you are finished, copy the data your partner collected in steps 4 and 5.

8. Draw a side-view diagram of the carton and the initial stream of water from each hole. Label the distance traveled by each stream.

9. If there is enough time left, you can check your results by having your partner hold the carton while you repeat the experiment.

	Top Hole	Middle Hole	Bottom Hole
Distance stream travels (cm)			
Shape & Direction of stream			
Diagram of all 3 streams			

Explain Your Results

1. Which streams of water traveled the least and greatest distances? What does the direction and distance traveled by each stream tell you about the stream's strength?

_____

_____

_____

_____

2. Is water pressure greater at the top of the carton or at the bottom of the carton? How do you know?

_____

_____

_____

Practice Forming Questions and Hypotheses

Forming questions and hypotheses means asking questions and suggesting possible answers, or *hypotheses,* that can be tested in an experiment. Often a hypothesis can be written by restating the question asked. In this activity, you will form and test your own hypothesis for a given question.

Materials

2 paper plates
ice cubes
table salt
clock or timer

What to Do

❶ Read and think about the question below. Then restate the question to form a hypothesis, or possible answer. Make sure your hypothesis can be tested using the materials listed above.

Question: Why do people sprinkle salt on icy sidewalks?

Hypothesis: _____

_____

❷ To test your hypothesis, find two ice cubes that are about the same size and that haven't started to melt yet (they should both look dry). Put each ice cube on a separate paper plate, and place both plates next to each other on a table.

❸ Sprinkle salt over one of the ice cubes, so the entire surface (top and sides) is covered.

❹ Check the time and record it as the "Starting Time" in the chart on page 20. Now watch both ice cubes closely to see what happens. Record your observations every two minutes.

❺ After ten minutes, compare the appearance of the two ice cubes.

	Ice	Ice with Salt
Starting Time:		
2 min.		
4 min.		
6 min.		
8 min.		
10 min.		
Final appearance:		

Explain Your Results

1. Based on your results, was your hypothesis correct? Explain.

_____

_____

2. The melting point of ice (solid water) is 32° Fahrenheit (0° Celsius). What must salt do to the melting point of ice to make the ice melt faster? Write your hypothesis, and explain your reasoning.

_____

_____

_____

© Pearson Education, Inc.

Practice Identifying and Controlling Variables

Identifying and controlling variables means changing one factor that may affect the outcome of an experiment, while keeping all other factors the same for each trial. The factor that is changed and tested is called the *independent variable*, the outcome of the experiment is the *dependent variable*, and the constant factors are the *controlled variables*. In this activity, you will perform an experiment and then identify the independent, dependent, and controlled variables.

Materials

horseshoe magnet
3 pieces of corrugated cardboard (10 cm × 10 cm)
3 paper clips
ruler

What to Do

1. Hold one piece of corrugated cardboard in front of you. Place the paper clips in a pile on the cardboard.

2. Hold the magnet directly under the cardboard. Try to use the magnet to drag the paper clips. Observe what happens. Record your observations in the chart.

3. Find the distance between the magnet and the paper clips by measuring the thickness of the cardboard. Record your measurements in the chart.

4. Now take two pieces of cardboard and stack them on top of one another.

5. Place the paper clips in the center of the two-layered cardboard piece. Repeat steps 2 and 3. Record your observations and measurements in the chart.

6. Add the third layer of corrugated cardboard. Repeat steps 2 and 3. Record your observations and measurements in the chart.

Pieces of Cardboard	Thickness of Cardboard	Results
1		
2		
3		

Explain Your Results

1. What is the purpose of this experiment?

_____

_____

2. What is the independent variable in this experiment?
What are the controlled variables? What is the dependent
variable?

_____

_____

_____

_____

3. Why does the magnet's strength get weaker when each
piece of cardboard is added?

_____

_____

Practice Making Operational Definitions

Making operational definitions means giving a unique description of or stating specific information about an object or event. You can use operational definitions to describe different objects or events according to your own observations and experiences. In this activity, you will add iodine to different kinds of food and make an operational definition of starch based on your results.

Materials

newspaper

plastic cup

iodine tincture

small pieces of raw potato, lettuce,
   banana, bread, and lunchmeat

water

tablespoon measure

eyedropper

What to Do

❶ The five food groups are bread/grain, fruit, vegetable, meat/protein, and dairy. Identify which food group potatoes, lettuce, bananas, bread, and lunchmeat belong to. Write your answers in the chart on page 24.

❷ Cover your desk or work area with several sheets of newspaper.

❸ Measure 2 tablespoons of iodine and 2 tablespoons of water into the plastic cup, and stir gently. Be careful not to spill any iodine, since it will leave a stain.

❹ Place a piece of raw potato on the newspaper.

❺ Use the eyedropper to place a few drops of the iodine and water solution on the potato. Wait a few minutes and observe what happens. Record your observations in the chart.

❻ Repeat steps 4 and 5 with the lettuce, banana, bread, and lunchmeat. Each time, make sure to wait a few minutes after applying the iodine, since some foods may take a little longer to show results.

❼ Throw the food away when you are finished.

© Pearson Education, Inc.

Food Item	Food Group	Observations (Reaction to Iodine)
Potato		
Banana		
Lettuce		
Bread		
Lunchmeat		

Explain Your Results

1. Many foods contain starch, a substance that we need to be healthy. Iodine reacts with starch by changing to a blue-black color. According to your results, which food groups are likely to contain starch? Explain your answers.

_____

_____

_____

2. Items other than food, such as paper, can also contain starch. Use your results to write an operational definition of starch that does not mention food groups.

_____

_____

Practice Investigating and Experimenting

Investigating and experimenting means carrying out a certain procedure, designed to answer a question and test a hypothesis. The results are used to form a conclusion. Sometimes the results are used to improve the experiment by changing it, or to design a new experiment. In this activity, you will conduct an experiment to test a hypothesis and investigate how your results can be tested in another experiment.

Materials

2 plastic cups (clear)   sheet of colored paper
teaspoon measure   water
ruler   sugar
scale or balance   table salt
measuring cup   clock or timer
black marker   paper towels for drying

What to Do

❶ Read the question: Which substance dissolves more quickly when stirred into water—sugar or salt? Write a hypothesis based on the question.

_____

_____

❷ Measure and weigh 1 teaspoon of salt and 1 teaspoon of sugar to see which substance is lighter. Make sure to level off the top of each filled teaspoon with a ruler or straight edge before weighing its contents. Record your observations in the chart on page 26.

❸ Use the black marker to label the two plastic cups "salt" and "sugar."

❹ Measure and pour 125 mL of water (room temperature) into each cup.

❺ Place both cups on the colored paper, so you can easily look at them at the same time. As each substance dissolves, you will be able to see more of the colored paper below the cup.

❻ Measure 1 teaspoon of salt exactly. Pour the teaspoon into the "salt" cup of water.

❼ Use the teaspoon to stir the salt and water for 10 seconds. Wait a few seconds and see if any salt has dissolved. Record your observations in the chart on page 26.

8 Record your observations after each 10 seconds of stirring. Keep stirring until all the salt has dissolved.

9 Now repeat steps 6, 7, and 8 with the sugar.

Hypothesis: Salt dissolves more quickly in water because it is lighter than sugar.

	Observations	Salt	Sugar
Weight	**Weight of 1 tsp (g)**		
	Which is lighter, salt or sugar? Check the correct box.		
Stirred into water	**After 10 seconds:**		
	After 20 seconds:		
	After 30 seconds:		
	After 40 seconds:		

Explain Your Results

1. Did your results prove the hypothesis to be true or false? Explain.

_____

_____

2. What do you think would happen if you did not stir the contents of each cup? State your hypothesis.

_____

_____

3. How would not stirring the contents of each cup change the procedure for the experiment?

_____

_____

_____

4. Now perform an experiment to test your hypothesis, using the procedure you described in question 3. Use the same cups you used for the first experiment, but make sure to wash them out well. Use the same amounts of water and salt or sugar as you did in the first experiment. Observe and record what happens every two minutes for eight minutes. Write your hypothesis and record your observations in the chart.

Hypothesis:		
Observations	**Salt**	**Sugar**
After 2 minutes:		
After 4 minutes:		
After 6 minutes:		
After 8 minutes:		

(Added to water)

5. Did your results prove the hypothesis to be true or false? Explain.

_____

_____

Explore: How can you classify seeds?

Classify your seeds. Sort them into 2 groups at each step using the property listed. Write the identity of each seed in the Identification Chart.

Identification Chart	
Seed	**Name**
Seed A	
Seed B	
Seed C	
Seed D	
Seed E	
Seed F	

Explain Your Results

List the properties you used to **classify** your seeds into groups. Identify each seed.

_____

_____

_____

_____

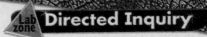
Self-Assessment Checklist	
I **observed** the seeds.	_____
I analyzed the seeds to determine their properties.	_____
I followed instructions to sort my seeds into two groups at each step using the property listed.	_____
I listed the properties I used to **classify** my seeds.	_____
I identified each seed.	_____

Notes for Home: Your child did an activity to **classify** and identify seeds.
Home Activity: With your child, list three properties you can use to **classify** vegetables into groups.

Investigate: What are some characteristics of yeast?

②-④ Use a hand lens to **observe** the yeast. Describe any changes.

Time	Appearance of Yeast on Watermelon Slice
After 1 hour	
After 2 hours	
After 3 hours	

❺ Observe a tiny amount of the yeast with a microscope. Draw your observations.

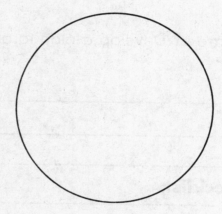

What tiny organisms did you see through the microscope?

_____

Explain Your Results

1. Did the appearance of the yeast change? How?

_____

_____

2. Yeast are not **classified** in the plant kingdom or the animal kingdom. Why?

_____

_____

_____

3. Infer: Which kind of bread has yeast added to its dough, flat bread or loaf bread? Why do you think so?

_____

_____

Go Further

Does yeast need light to grow? Develop a plan to answer this or other questions you may have.

_____

_____

Self-Assessment Checklist	
I followed instructions to prepare the watermelon slice and put it inside the bag.	_____
I used a hand lens to **observe** the yeast every hour and **recorded data** in the chart.	_____
I **observed** a tiny amount of the yeast with a microscope and drew my observations.	_____
I explained why yeast are not **classified** in the plant kingdom or the animal kingdom.	_____
I made an **inference** about which bread is made with yeast added to its dough and explained my answer.	_____

 Notes for Home: Your child did an activity to **observe** some characteristics of yeast.
Home Activity: With your child, discuss other fungi and how they are similar to yeast.

© Pearson Education, Inc.

Lab Zone Activity

How does water move through nonvascular plants?

Materials

bowl of water and food coloring

straw and dropper

string

waxed paper

What to Do

1. Put a few drops of food coloring in the water. Stir the water with the straw.

2. Gather the string into a pile. Place it on the waxed paper.

3. Set the water next to the waxed paper.

4. Pull one end of the string from the pile. Place the end in the water. Make sure that you place it far enough in the water so that it doesn't pull out of the water.

5. **Observe** the string closest to the water for at least 15 minutes. Record your observations.

Process Skills

You can use your **observations** from this activity to make an **inference** about the movement of water in nonvascular plants.

Explain Your Results

1. How did the string change as you observed it? What caused this change?

2. **Infer** Use what you observed in this activity to explain how water moves through nonvascular plants.

Activity

Lab zone

How are molds alike and different?

Materials

moldy fruit

moldy bread

hand lens

What to Do

1. Look through the plastic bag to **observe** the mold on the piece of fruit. Describe what you see. Be sure to describe the color and texture of the mold, the pattern that it makes on the fruit, and any other characteristics that you see. If more than one kind of mold grows on the fruit, be sure to record observations about each.

Be careful! Do not open the bag.

2. Use the hand lens to examine each mold. Draw each mold and describe its characteristics.

3. Repeat steps 1 and 2 with the bread mold.

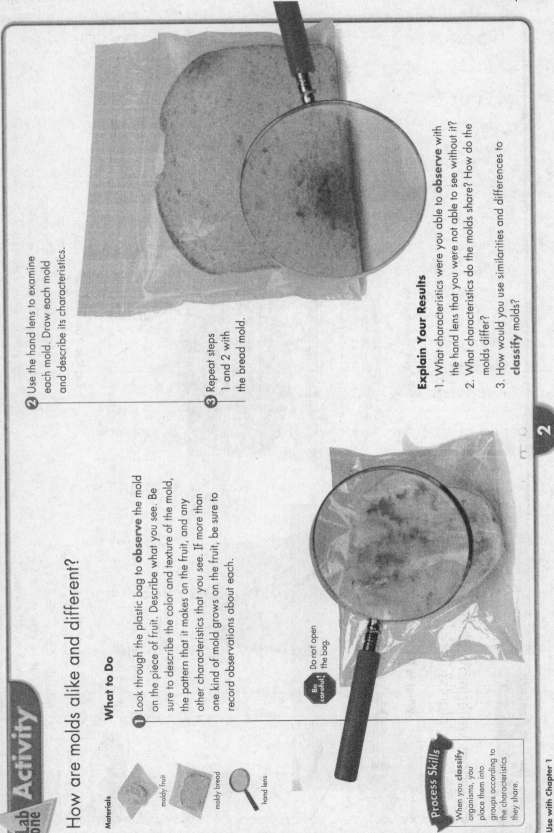

Explain Your Results

1. What characteristics were you able to **observe** with the hand lens that you were not able to see without it?

2. What characteristics do the molds share? How do the molds differ?

3. How would you use similarities and differences to **classify** molds?

Process Skills

When you **classify** organisms, you place them into groups according to the characteristics they share.

How does water move through nonvascular plants?

Explain Your Results

1. How did the string change as you observed it? What caused this change?

_____

_____

2. Infer: Use what you observed in this activity to explain how water moves through nonvascular plants.

_____

_____

Self-Assessment Checklist	
I followed instructions to put the food coloring in the bowl and stir the water with the straw.	____
I followed instructions to place the end of the string in the water.	____
I **observed** the string for 15 minutes and recorded my **observations.**	____
I explained how the string changed as I **observed** it and what caused this change.	____
I made an **inference** about how water moves through nonvascular plants.	____

Notes for Home: Your child did an activity to **observe** how water moves through nonvascular plants.
Home Activity: With your child, discuss the differences between vascular and nonvascular plants.

How are molds alike and different?

1 Look through the plastic bag to **observe** the mold on the piece of fruit. Describe what you see. Be sure to describe the color and texture of the mold, the pattern that it makes on the fruit, and any other characteristics that you see. If more than one kind of mold grows on the fruit, be sure to record observations about each.

_____

_____

2 Now use the hand lens to examine each mold. Draw each mold and describe its characteristics.

_____

_____

3 Repeat steps 1 and 2 with the bread mold.

_____

_____

© Pearson Education, Inc.

_____

_____

Explain Your Results

1. What characteristics were you able to **observe** with the hand lens that you were not able to see without it?

_____

_____

2. What characteristics do the molds share? How do the molds differ?

_____

_____

3. How would you use similarities and differences to **classify** molds?

_____

_____

Self-Assessment Checklist	
I **observed** the mold on the piece of fruit and described and drew what I saw.	_____
I **observed** the mold on the bread and described and drew what I saw.	_____
I named the characteristics **observed** with the hand lens.	_____
I described the characteristics the molds share and how they differ.	_____
I explained how to use similarities and differences to **classify** molds.	_____

Notes for Home: Your child did an activity to **observe** how molds are alike and how they are different.
Home Activity: With your child, find more pictures of mold online or in the library and compare them to the mold studied in class.

Explore: What do yeast cells need to grow?

❷ Observe the cups every 15 minutes for 1 hour. Record your **observations**.

	15 minutes	30 minutes	45 minutes	1 hour
Cup 1: Yeast, water, sugar				
Cup 2: Yeast, sugar				
Cup 3: Yeast, water				

Explain Your Results

1. Observe: What happened to the contents of each cup?

_____

_____

2. Infer: What materials are needed for yeast cells to grow?

_____

_____

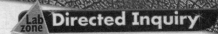
Self-Assessment Checklist

I followed instructions to put yeast, water, and sugar in the correct cups. _____

I **observed** each cup every 15 minutes. _____

I recorded my **observations** in the chart. _____

I described what happened to the contents of each cup. _____

I made an **inference** about what materials yeast need to grow. _____

Notes for Home: Your child did an activity to discover what yeast cells need to grow.
Home Activity: With your child, discuss why chefs test yeast to make sure it is alive before adding it to bread dough.

Name _____

Investigate: How can you make a model arm?

❹–❺ Observe how the model arm moves when you pull each string. Record what you observe.

String Pulled	How the Model Arm Moved
Biceps string pulled	
Triceps string pulled	

Explain Your Results

1. What happens in your **model** when you pull each piece of yarn?

_____

_____

2. How are your model and a real arm alike and different?

_____

_____

_____

_____

_____

_____

Go Further

How can you make a model that shows how the muscular and skeletal systems work together in the leg? Make a plan to find out.

_____

_____

_____

_____

Self-Assessment Checklist	
I followed the diagram on the Model Arm Pattern to make a model arm.	_____
I moved the model arm by pulling each string.	
I **observed** the movements of the model arm.	_____
I recorded my **observations** in a chart.	
I **communicated** how my model is like a real arm and how it is different.	_____

 Notes for Home: Your child did an activity to make a model of how biceps and triceps move the lower arm.
Home Activity: With your child, discuss how the muscles in your thigh work to bend and straighten your leg.

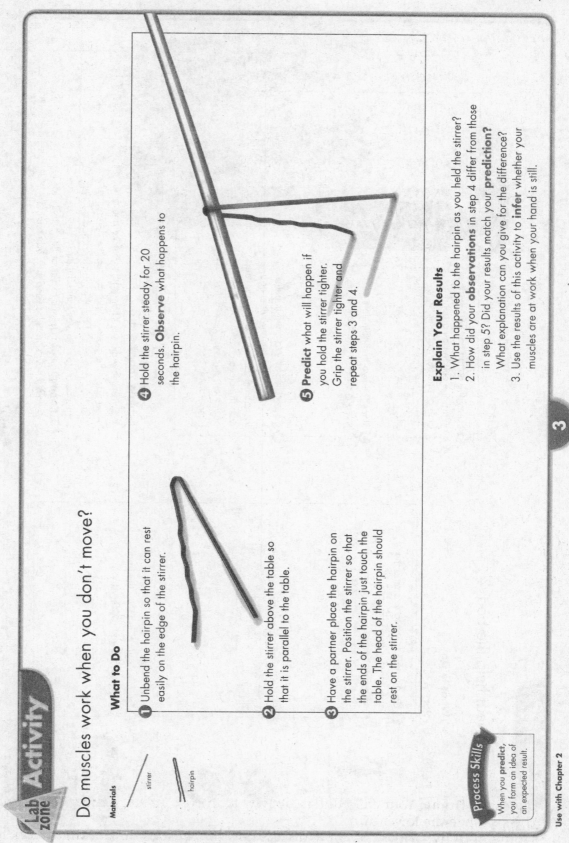

Lab zone Activity

Do muscles work when you don't move?

Materials

stirrer

hairpin

What to Do

1. Unbend the hairpin so that it can rest easily on the edge of the stirrer.

2. Hold the stirrer above the table so that it is parallel to the table.

3. Have a partner place the hairpin on the stirrer. Position the stirrer so that the ends of the hairpin just touch the table. The head of the hairpin should rest on the stirrer.

4. Hold the stirrer steady for 20 seconds. **Observe** what happens to the hairpin.

5. **Predict** what will happen if you hold the stirrer tighter. Grip the stirrer tighter and repeat steps 3 and 4.

Explain Your Results

1. What happened to the hairpin as you held the stirrer?

2. How did your **observations** in step 4 differ from those in step 5? Did your results match your **prediction?** What explanation can you give for the difference?

3. Use the results of this activity to **infer** whether your muscles are at work when your hand is still.

Process Skills

When you **predict,** you form an idea of an expected result.

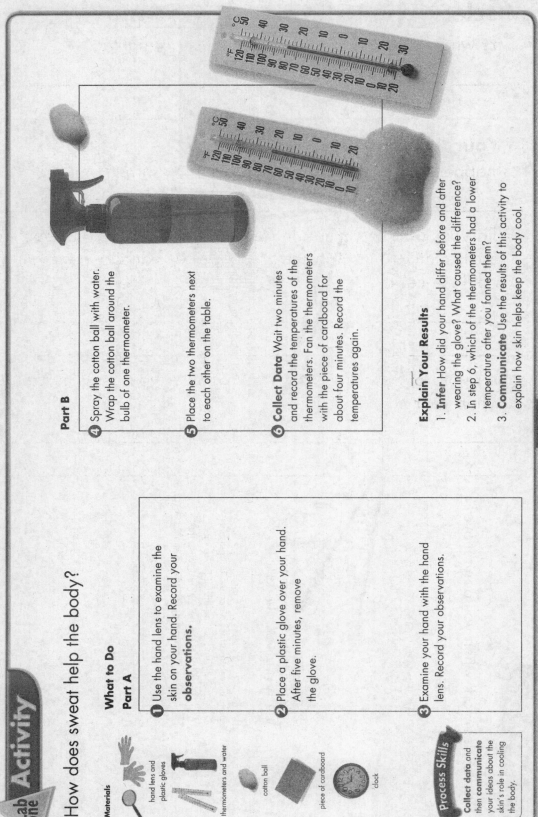

Lab zone Activity

How does sweat help the body?

Materials

hand lens and
plastic gloves

thermometers and water

cotton ball

piece of cardboard

clock

Process Skills

Collect data and
then **communicate**
your ideas about the
skin's role in cooling
the body.

What to Do

Part A

1. Use the hand lens to examine the skin on your hand. Record your **observations.**

2. Place a plastic glove over your hand. After five minutes, remove the glove.

3. Examine your hand with the hand lens. Record your observations.

Part B

4. Spray the cotton ball with water. Wrap the cotton ball around the bulb of one thermometer.

5. Place the two thermometers next to each other on the table.

6. **Collect Data** Wait two minutes and record the temperatures of the thermometers. Fan the thermometers with the piece of cardboard for about four minutes. Record the temperatures again.

Explain Your Results

1. **Infer** How did your hand differ before and after wearing the glove? What caused the difference?

2. In step 6, which of the thermometers had a lower temperature after you fanned them?

3. **Communicate** Use the results of this activity to explain how skin helps keep the body cool.

4

Do muscles work when you don't move?

⑤ Predict what will happen if you hold the stirrer tighter.

_____

_____

Explain Your Results

1. What happened to the hairpin as you held the stirrer?

_____

2. How did your **observations** in step 4 differ from those in step 5? Did your results match your **prediction?** What explanation can you give for the difference?

_____

_____

3. Use the results of this activity to **infer** whether your muscles are at work when your hand is still.

_____

_____

Self-Assessment Checklist

I held the stirrer steady for 20 seconds and **observed** what happened to the hairpin. _____

I **predicted** what would happen if I held the stirrer tighter and tested my **prediction.** _____

I described what happened to the hairpin during the experiment. _____

I explained whether my **observations** in step 4 matched those in step 5. _____

I made an **inference** about whether muscles are at work when a hand is still. _____

Notes for Home: Your child did an activity to **observe** whether or not muscles work when you're not moving.
Home Activity: With your child, discuss what happens in your body when you move a muscle.

How does sweat help the body?

❶ Use the hand lens to examine the skin on your hand. Record your **observations**.

_____

❷—❸ Place a plastic glove over your hand. After five minutes, remove the glove. Examine your hand with the hand lens. Record your observations.

_____

❻ Collect Data: Wait two minutes and record the temperatures of the thermometers. Fan the thermometers with the piece of cardboard for about 4 minutes. Then record the temperatures again.

	Initial Temperature	**Temperature After Fanning with Cardboard**
Thermometer with Cotton Ball		
Thermometer without Cotton Ball		

Explain Your Results

1. Infer: How did your hand differ before and after wearing the glove? What caused the difference?

_____

_____

2. In step 6, which of the thermometers had a lower temperature after you fanned them?

_____

3. Communicate: Use the results of this activity to explain how skin helps keep the body cool.

_____

_____

Self-Assessment Checklist	
I **observed** the skin on my hand before and after wearing the plastic glove.	_____
I followed instructions to spray the cotton ball with water and wrap it around a thermometer.	_____
I **collected data** about the temperature of the thermometers before and after fanning.	_____
I made an **inference** about what caused the difference before and after wearing the glove.	_____
I **communicated** how skin helps keep the body cool.	_____

Notes for Home: Your child did an activity to **observe** how sweat helps keep the body cool.
Home Activity: With your child, exercise to build up a sweat and then **observe** the process studied in the activity.

Explore: How can you observe your pulse?

Explain Your Results

1. Describe the movements of the straw you **observed.**

_____

2. Infer: What caused the straw to move?

_____

Self-Assessment Checklist	
I followed instructions to prepare the straw.	_____
I followed instructions to place the bottom of the clay on my wrist.	_____
I **observed** the movement of the straw.	_____
I described the movements of the straw I **observed.**	_____
I **inferred** what caused the straw to move.	_____

Notes for Home: Your child did an activity to **observe** the pulsation of blood vessels in the wrist.
Home Activity: With your child, use your fingers to **observe** the pulsation of blood vessels on the side of your neck.

Investigate: What is your lung capacity?

②–④ Blow through the straw to form a bubble. **Measure** the diameter of the ring left on the bag. Use the chart on page 81 of your book to **estimate** the amount of air you exhale. Repeat for each student in your group. **Record** your **data** in the chart.

Name of Student	Diameter of Ring (centimeters)	Lung Capacity (liters)

Explain Your Results

1. When you blow into the straw, what happens to the air you breathe in?

_____

2. Infer: Why were there differences in the diameters of the rings for different students?

_____

Go Further

Does posture affect how much air you can breathe in and out? With your teacher's permission, make and carry out a plan to investigate this or another question.

_____

_____

_____

_____

Guided Inquiry

Self-Assessment Checklist	
I followed instructions to prepare the garbage bag.	_____
I blew as much breath as I could into the straw and **observed** the formation of a bubble.	_____
I **measured** the ring left behind and used the chart to **estimate** the air exhaled.	_____
I recorded the diameter of the ring and lung capacity of each student in my group.	_____
I made an **inference** about why there are differences in the diameters of the rings.	_____

Notes for Home: Your child did an activity to **measure** the amount of air exhaled from the lungs.
Home Activity: With your child, discuss how age and height might affect lung capacity.

© Pearson Education, Inc.

Lab zone **Activity**

How hard does your heart work?

Materials

newspaper

water

containers

measuring cup

clock

What to Do

1 Spread several sheets of newspaper on top of a table.

2 Use the pitcher to fill one container about three-quarters full with water. Leave the other container empty. Place the containers on the newspaper next to each other.

Be careful!

Clean up spills as they occur.

3 Use the measuring cup to transfer water from one bowl to the other. Try not to spill any of the water. Count each time you transfer water and try to make 80 transfers of water in one minute. Use the clock to time your progress.

4 Repeat step 3 until you can make about 80 transfers in one minute.

5

Explain Your Results

1. **Estimate** Your heart beats about 80 times a minute. Each time your heart beats, it pumps about $\frac{1}{4}$ cup of blood. About how much blood does your heart pump in one minute?

2. In your **model**, were you able to work as hard as your heart?

3. How did your model help you understand how much work your heart does?

Process Skills

You can use a **model** to help you estimate how hard your heart works.

Name _____

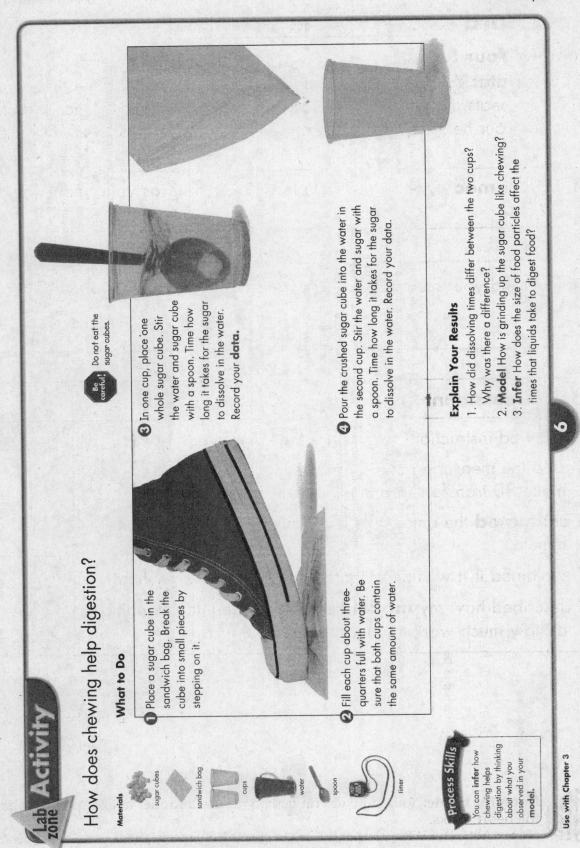

Lab zone Activity

How does chewing help digestion?

Materials

sugar cubes

sandwich bag

cups

water

spoon

timer

What to Do

1. Place a sugar cube in the sandwich bag. Break the cube into small pieces by stepping on it.

2. Fill each cup about three-quarters full with water. Be sure that both cups contain the same amount of water.

Be careful! Do not eat the sugar cubes.

3. In one cup, place one whole sugar cube. Stir the water and sugar cube with a spoon. Time how long it takes for the sugar to dissolve in the water. Record your **data**.

4. Pour the crushed sugar cube into the water in the second cup. Stir the water and sugar with a spoon. Time how long it takes for the sugar to dissolve in the water. Record your data.

Explain Your Results

1. How did dissolving times differ between the two cups? Why was there a difference?

2. **Model** How is grinding up the sugar cube like chewing?

3. **Infer** How does the size of food particles affect the times that liquids take to digest food?

Process Skills

You can **infer** how chewing helps digestion by thinking about what you observed in your **model**.

How hard does your heart work?

Explain Your Results

1. Estimate: Your heart beats about 80 times a minute. Each time your heart beats, it pumps about $\frac{1}{4}$ cup of blood. About how much blood does your heart pump in one minute?

_____

2. In your **model,** were you able to work as hard as your heart?

_____

_____

3. How did your model help you understand how much work your heart does?

_____

Self-Assessment Checklist	
I followed instructions to prepare the containers.	_____
I used the measuring cup to transfer water and tried to make 80 transfers in one minute.	_____
I **estimated** the amount of blood my heart pumps in one minute.	_____
I explained if it was possible to work as hard as my heart.	_____
I described how my **model** helped provide understanding of how much work my heart does.	_____

Notes for Home: Your child did an activity to **use a model** to examine how hard the heart works.
Home Activity: With your child, try to count how many times your heart beats in one minute.

How does chewing help digestion?

3–4 In one cup, place one whole sugar cube. Stir the water and sugar cube with a spoon. Time how long it takes for the sugar to dissolve in the water. Record your **data.** Pour the crushed sugar cube into the water in the second cup. Stir the water and sugar with a spoon. Time how long it takes for the sugar to dissolve in the water. Record your data.

	Time It Takes to Dissolve (min. and sec.)
Whole Sugar Cube	
Crushed Sugar Cube	

Explain Your Results

1. How did dissolving times differ between the two cups? Was there a difference?

_____

_____

2. Model: How is grinding up the sugar cube like chewing?

_____

_____

3. Infer: How does the size of food particles affect the times the liquids take to digest food?

_____

Self-Assessment Checklist	
I followed instructions to crush a sugar cube and fill two cups with water.	_____
I recorded **data** about how long it took the sugar cubes to dissolve in water.	_____
I explained how dissolving times differed between the two cups.	_____
I described how grinding up the sugar cube is a **model** of chewing.	_____
I made an **inference** about how the size of food particles affects the time to digest food.	_____

Notes for Home: Your child did an activity to **model** how chewing affects digestion.
Home Activity: With your child, discuss the path that food takes through the body.

Explore: What color can come from leaves?

4 Predict the color that will come from the leaves.

_____

Observe the strip after 15 minutes.

_____

_____

Explain Your Results

Explain the reasons for your **prediction.** Was your prediction accurate?

_____

_____

Self-Assessment Checklist	
I followed instructions to prepare the cup.	
I **predicted** the color that would come from the leaves.	_____
I **observed** the strip after 15 minutes.	_____
I explained the reasons for my **prediction.**	_____
I determined whether my **prediction** was accurate.	_____

Notes for Home: Your child did an activity to find out what color can come from leaves.
Home Activity: With your child, discuss what causes leaves to turn brown when plants die.

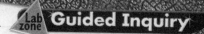
Investigate: Does the direction seeds are planted affect the direction roots grow?

❹-❺ Observe the seeds daily for a week. Draw and describe how the roots grew.

Position of Bean (Describe the position of bean seed)	Direction of Roots
Bean 1	
Bean 2	
Bean 3	
Bean 4	

Explain Your Results

1. What direction did the roots grow?

_____

2. Interpret Data: What might you conclude about the effect of gravity on the growth of roots?

_____

_____

Go Further

What other factors affect how a plant grows? Develop a plan to find out what factors affect the growth, health, or reproduction of bean plants.

_____

_____

_____

Self-Assessment Checklist

I followed instructions to prepare a cup with seeds in the correct positions. _____

I **observed** the seeds daily for a week. _____

I drew and described the growth of the roots in the chart. _____

I **observed** the direction the roots grew. _____

I **interpreted data** to draw a conclusion about the effect of gravity on the growth of roots. _____

Notes for Home: Your child did an activity to find out whether the direction seeds are planted affects the direction their roots grow.
Home Activity: With your child, discuss why the stems and leaves of plants grow up instead of down.

© Pearson Education, Inc.

Lab zone Activity

How does placement affect the amount of light a leaf receives?

Materials

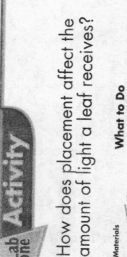

2 straws

green construction paper

scissors and tape

clay

flashlight

Process Skills

Making and using **models** can help you understand how leaves are arranged to get the most light.

What to Do

1 Use the straw as the stem of a plant. Use the green paper for the leaves. Cut out six leaves that are about the same size and shape.

2 Tape the leaves on the straw so they look like the leaves in the picture.

3 Place your **model** in the clay so that it stands upright. Hold the flashlight directly above your model plant. **Observe** and record where the light falls on the leaves.

7

4 Think about how the leaves could be arranged so that they all receive the same amount of light. Draw a picture of your idea.

5 Use a straw, more construction paper leaves, and the tape to make the plant you planned in your drawing.

6 Repeat step 3.

Explain Your Results

1. **Observe** Did all of the leaves in step 3 receive the same amount of light? Which leaves in your **model** received the most light?

2. Did all of the leaves in step 6 receive the same amount of light? How could the leaves be arranged to receive the most light?

Activity Book

Lab zone Activity

How do monocot and dicot seeds differ?

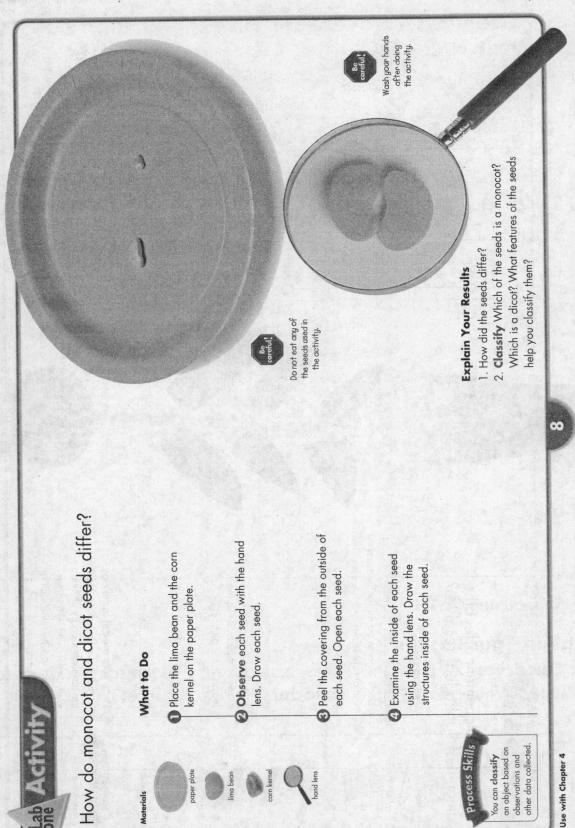

Materials

paper plate

lima bean

corn kernel

hand lens

What to Do

① Place the lima bean and the corn kernel on the paper plate.

② **Observe** each seed with the hand lens. Draw each seed.

③ Peel the covering from the outside of each seed. Open each seed.

④ Examine the inside of each seed using the hand lens. Draw the structures inside of each seed.

Be careful!
Do not eat any of the seeds used in the activity.

Be careful!
Wash your hands after doing the activity.

Explain Your Results

1. How did the seeds differ?

2. **Classify** Which of the seeds is a monocot? Which is a dicot? What features of the seeds help you classify them?

Process Skills

You can **classify** an object based on observations and other data collected.

8

Name _____

Activity Flip Chart

Use with page 7

How does leaf placement affect the amount of light it receives?

3 Place your model in the clay so that it stands upright. Hold the flashlight directly above your model plant. Observe and record where the light falls on the leaves.

	Observations
Trial 1	
Trial 2	

4 Think about how the leaves could be arranged so that they all receive the same amount of light. Draw a picture of your idea.

6 Repeat step 3.

Explain Your Results

1. Observe: Did all of the leaves in step 3 receive the same amount of light? Which leaves in your **model** received the most light?

_____

_____

© Pearson Education, Inc.

Activity Book

Activity Flip Chart **65**

2. Did all of the leaves in step 6 receive the same amount of light? How could the leaves be arranged to receive the most light?

_____

_____

Self-Assessment Checklist	
I followed instructions to make a **model** of a plant.	_____
I held the flashlight above my **model** plant and **observed** and recorded where the light fell.	_____
I thought about how the leaves could be placed so that they receive the same amount of light.	_____
I drew a picture of my idea.	_____
I made the new plant and then repeated the test.	_____

Notes for Home: Your child did an activity to **make a model** to see how leaf placement affects the amount of light a plant receives.
Home Activity: With your child, **observe** plants in your neighborhood and notice how they have placed their leaves.

How do monocot and dicot seeds differ?

2 **Observe** each seed with the hand lens. Draw each seed.

4 Examine the inside of each seed using the hand lens. Draw the structures inside of each seed.

Explain Your Results

1. How did the seeds differ?

_____

2. Classify: Which of the seeds is a monocot? Which is a dicot? What features of the seeds help you classify them?

_____

Self-Assessment Checklist	
I followed instructions to place the lima bean and the corn kernel on the paper plate.	_____
I **observed** each seed using the hand lens and sketched each seed.	_____
I examined the inside of each seed using the hand lens and drew the structures inside.	_____
I explained how the seeds differ.	_____
I **classified** the seeds as monocots or dicots and explained what features help **classify** them.	_____

Notes for Home: Your child did an activity to **observe** how monocot and dicot seeds differ.
Home Activity: Have your child explain to you how to tell the difference between full-grown monocot and dicot plants.

Explore: How can you find out how many animals live in an area?

1 Scatter 2 handfuls of cereal on a checkerboard. Guess how many pieces of cereal there are.

_____

2 Find an **estimate** of the total number of pieces:
Count the number of pieces on 4 squares:

_____

Divide by 4.

_____

Multiply your answer by the total number of squares to find an **estimate** of the total number of pieces.

_____

3 Count all the pieces of cereal on the checkerboard.

_____

Explain Your Results

1. Which was easiest: guessing, estimating, or counting? Which was most accurate?

_____

2. How do you think you could make your **estimate** more accurate?

_____

_____

Self-Assessment Checklist	
I followed instructions to scatter cereal and guess how many pieces there were.	_____
I **estimated** the total number of pieces of cereal.	_____
I counted all of the pieces of cereal on the checkerboard.	_____
I determined the easiest method of finding how many animals live in an area.	_____
I drew conclusions about how to make my **estimate** more accurate.	_____

Notes for Home: Your child did an activity to **estimate** the number of objects in a population.

Home Activity: With your child, discuss how you would accurately estimate the number of people who live in your neighborhood or town.

Investigate: How can you show that plants use carbon dioxide?

❶-❹ Record how the water changes color.

	Color of Water with BTB
Before breathing out into the water	
After breathing out into the water	
After adding elodea to the water	

Explain Your Results

1. What made the color of the water change when you breathed into it?

_____

_____

_____

2. In your **investigation,** what made the color change after you added the elodea?

_____

_____

_____

Go Further

What would happen if the elodea and water with BTB were put in a dark place? Write a procedure others could follow to answer this question.

_____

_____

_____

_____

Self-Assessment Checklist	
I followed instructions to **investigate** whether plants use carbon dioxide.	_____
I breathed gently through the straw and **observed** the water change color.	_____
I added elodea to the cup and **observed** the water change color.	_____
I **recorded data** about the changes I **observed.**	_____
I drew conclusions about what made the color change.	

Notes for Home: Your child did an activity to **investigate** whether plants use carbon dioxide.
Home Activity: With your child, discuss why only green plants use carbon dioxide.

Activity Book

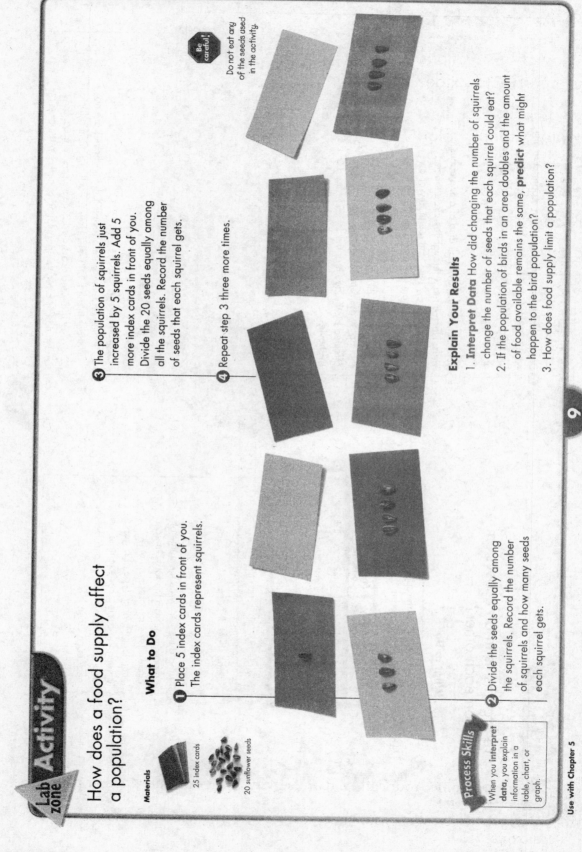

© Pearson Education, Inc.

Lab zone Activity

How does a food supply affect a population?

Materials

25 index cards

20 sunflower seeds

What to Do

1. Place 5 index cards in front of you. The index cards represent squirrels.

2. Divide the seeds equally among the squirrels. Record the number of squirrels and how many seeds each squirrel gets.

3. The population of squirrels just increased by 5 squirrels. Add 5 more index cards in front of you. Divide the 20 seeds equally among all the squirrels. Record the number of seeds that each squirrel gets.

4. Repeat step 3 three more times.

Be careful!

Do not eat any of the seeds used in the activity.

Explain Your Results

1. **Interpret Data** How did changing the number of squirrels change the number of seeds that each squirrel could eat?

2. If the population of birds in an area doubles and the amount of food available remains the same, **predict** what might happen to the bird population?

3. How does food supply limit a population?

Process Skills

When you interpret **data**, you explain information in a table, chart, or graph.

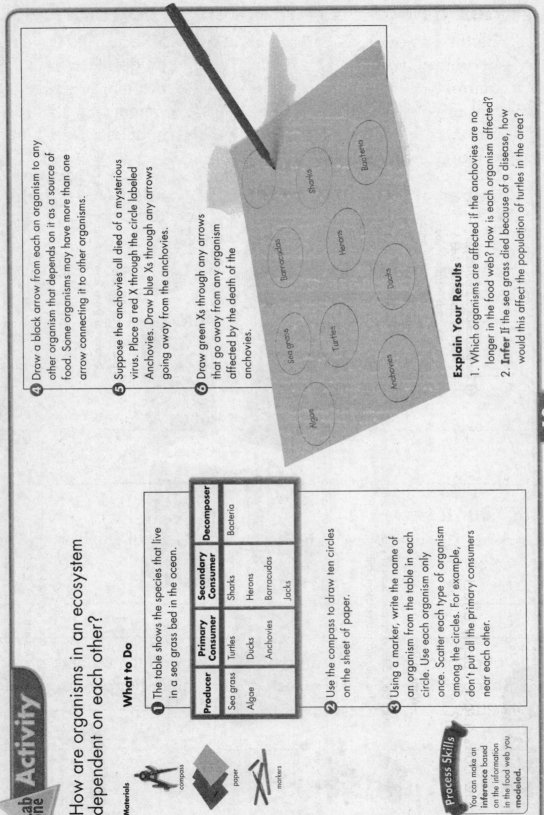

Activity

How are organisms in an ecosystem dependent on each other?

Materials

compass

paper

markers

What to Do

1. The table shows the species that live in a sea grass bed in the ocean.

Producer	Primary Consumer	Secondary Consumer	Decomposer
Sea grass	Turtles	Sharks	Bacteria
Algae	Ducks	Herons	
	Anchovies	Barracudas	
		Jacks	

2. Use the compass to draw ten circles on the sheet of paper.

3. Using a marker, write the name of an organism from the table in each circle. Use each organism only once. Scatter each type of organism among the circles. For example, don't put all the primary consumers near each other.

Process Skills

You can make an inference based on the information in the food web you modeled.

4. Draw a black arrow from each an organism to any other organism that depends on it as a source of food. Some organisms may have more than one arrow connecting it to other organisms.

5. Suppose the anchovies all died of a mysterious virus. Place a red X through the circle labeled Anchovies. Draw blue Xs through any arrows going away from the anchovies.

6. Draw green Xs through any arrows that go away from any organism affected by the death of the anchovies.

Explain Your Results

1. Which organisms are affected if the anchovies are no longer in the food web? How is each organism affected?

2. **Infer** If the sea grass died because of a disease, how would this affect the population of turtles in the area?

10

How does a food supply affect a population?

2–4 Divide the seeds equally among the squirrels. Record the number of squirrels and how many seeds each squirrel gets. The population of squirrels just increased by 5 squirrels. Add 5 more index cards in front of you. Divide the 20 seeds equally among the squirrels. Record the number of seeds that each squirrel gets. Repeat step 3 three more times.

Number of Squirrels	Number of Seeds per Squirrel

Explain Your Results

1. Interpret Data: How did changing the number of squirrels change the number of seeds that each squirrel could eat?

_____

_____

2. If the population of birds in an area doubles and the amount of food available remains the same, **predict** what might happen to the bird population?

_____

3. How does food supply limit a population?

_____

_____

Self-Assessment Checklist	
I divided the seeds equally among the squirrels and recorded how many each squirrel got.	_____
I added five squirrels at a time and recorded the number of seeds each squirrel got.	_____
I **interpreted my data** to find how the number of seeds each squirrel could eat changed.	_____
I **predicted** what might happen if a bird population doubles but the food supply is the same.	_____
I explained how food supply limits a population.	_____

Notes for Home: Your child did an activity to examine how a food supply affects a population.
Home Activity: With your child, discuss what might happen to the squirrels if chipmunks that eat the same seeds start moving into the community.

© Pearson Education, Inc.

How are organisms in an ecosystem dependent on each other?

Explain Your Results

1. Which organisms are affected if the anchovies are no longer in the food web? How is each organism affected?

_____

_____

_____

2. Infer: If the sea grass died because of a disease, how would this affect the population of turtles in the area?

_____

Self-Assessment Checklist	
I followed instructions to draw circles on the paper and write in the names of the organisms.	_____
I drew black arrows from each organism to any other organism that depended on it for food.	_____
I drew Xs through the animals that would be affected if all the anchovies died.	_____
I explained how the organisms would be affected if the anchovies died.	_____
I made an **inference** about how the death of the seagrass would affect the population of turtles.	_____

Notes for Home: Your child did an activity to examine how organisms in an ecosystem are dependent on each other.
Home Activity: With your child, discuss what organisms humans depend on.

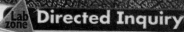
Explore: How can pollution affect a habitat?

4 **Observe** what happens to the yeast in the cups after 5, 10, and
15 minutes. View the cups from the side.

5 minutes: _____

10 minutes: _____

15 minutes: _____

Explain Your Results

1. What happened to the yeast in each cup?

_____

_____

2. Infer: Pollution can harm or even kill living things. Which cup
represents the polluted habitat? Explain your answer.

_____

Self-Assessment Checklist

I followed instructions to pour water and vinegar into the cups and add yeast.	_____
I **observed** what happened to the yeast every 5 minutes for 15 minutes.	_____
I described what happened to the yeast in each cup.	_____
I made an **inference** about which cup represented the polluted habitat and explained my answer.	_____
I explained the basis for my **inference.**	_____

Notes for Home: Your child did an activity to observe the effect of a pollutant on a habitat.
Home Activity: With your child, discuss 3 sources of water pollution.

Investigate: What happens when a wetland ecosystem changes?

5-6 Predict how the wetland will change from Day 3 to Day 13. Record your predictions. **Observe** the wetland every 2 days and record how it changes.

	Predictions	**Observed Changes**
Day 3		
Day 5		
Day 7		
Day 9		
Day 11		
Day 13		

Explain Your Results

1. What changes did you **observe** in the wetland?

_____

2. How did the changes you observed compare to your **predictions?**

_____

_____

Go Further

How could you make a model to show how a wetland can help prevent floods or erosion? Make a plan to answer this or other questions you may have.

_____

_____

_____

Self-Assessment Checklist	
I followed instructions to make a wetland.	_____
I stayed on task during the activity.	_____
I **predicted** how the wetland would change and recorded my **predictions** in the chart.	_____
I **observed** the wetland every two days and recorded my **observations** in the chart.	_____
I compared the changes I **observed** to my **predictions.**	_____

Notes for Home: Your child did an activity to **predict** and **observe** natural causes of changes in a wetland ecosystem.
Home Activity: With your child, discuss how changes in climate can affect an ecosystem.

Lab zone Activity

How do brine shrimp react to light?

Materials

brine shrimp in jar

black construction paper

scissors and tape

metric ruler

flashlight

clock

What to Do

1 **Observe** the brine shrimp in the jar. Record how the shrimp are scattered around the jar.

2 Measure and cut the black construction paper so that it will completely cover the outside of the jar.

3 Cut a small square window in the paper that will be near the bottom of the jar. Make the window about 1 cm on each side.

4 Tape the paper so that it covers the jar. Make sure the window is near the bottom.

5 Place a flashlight over the window. Shine the flashlight in the window for three minutes. Then quickly remove the paper and **observe** where the brine shrimp are located. Record your observations.

6 After two minutes, cover the jar again. This time, place the window near the top of the jar. Repeat step 5.

Explain Your Results

1. How did the brine shrimp react to the light?

2. How do you know that the brine shrimp reacted to the light and not gravity?

3. **Infer** where brine shrimp live in the ocean. Do you think they live in the deep ocean or in shallow pools near the shore? Why?

Process Skills

When you **observe**, you use your senses to gather information.

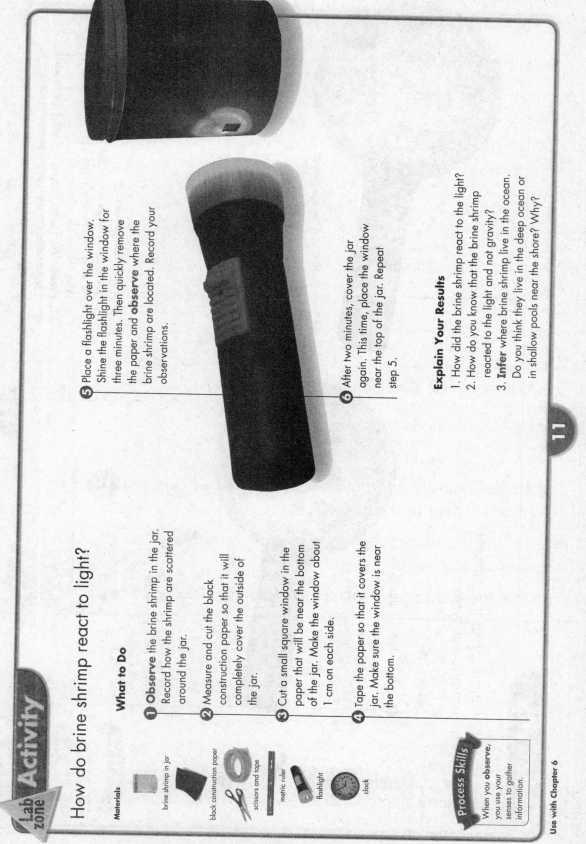

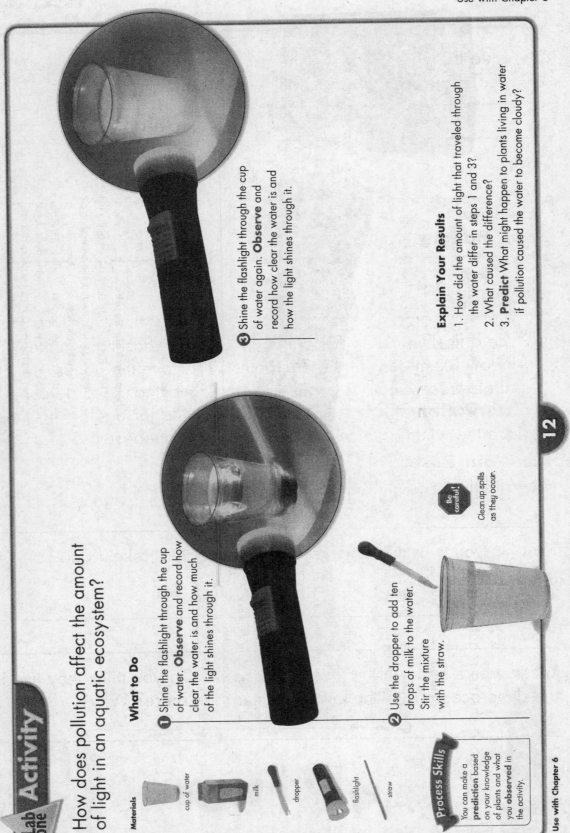

Lab zone Activity

How does pollution affect the amount of light in an aquatic ecosystem?

Materials

cup of water

milk

dropper

flashlight

straw

What to Do

1. Shine the flashlight through the cup of water. **Observe** and record how clear the water is and how much of the light shines through it.

2. Use the dropper to add ten drops of milk to the water. Stir the mixture with the straw.

Be careful!

Clean up spills as they occur.

3. Shine the flashlight through the cup of water again. **Observe** and record how clear the water is and how the light shines through it.

Process Skills

You can make a **prediction** based on your knowledge of plants and what you **observed** in the activity.

Explain Your Results

1. How did the amount of light that traveled through the water differ in steps 1 and 3?

2. What caused the difference?

3. **Predict** What might happen to plants living in water if pollution caused the water to become cloudy?

How do brine shrimp react to light?

1 **Observe** the brine shrimp in the jar. Record how the shrimp are scattered throughout the jar.

	Shrimp Positions
Start	
Window Near Bottom	
Window Near Top	

5–6 Place a flashlight over the window. Shine the flashlight in the window for three minutes. Then quickly remove the paper and observe where the brine shrimp are located. Record your **observations.** After two minutes, cover the jar again. This time, place the window near the top of the jar. Repeat step 5.

Explain Your Results

1. How did the brine shrimp react to the light?

_____

2. How do you know that the brine shrimp reacted to light and not gravity?

_____

_____

3. Infer where brine shrimp live in the ocean. Do you think they live in the deep ocean or in shallow pools near the shore? Why?

_____

Self-Assessment Checklist	
I **observed** the brine shrimp and recorded how they were scattered throughout the jar.	_____
I placed the window near the bottom and **observed** where the brine shrimp were located.	_____
I placed the window near the top and **observed** where the brine shrimp were located.	_____
I explained how it was clear that the brine shrimp reacted to light and not gravity.	_____
I made an **inference** about where brine shrimp live in the ocean.	_____

Notes for Home: Your child did an activity to **observe** how brine shrimp react to light.
Home Activity: With your child, name 2 other animals that would have a reaction to light.

Activity Book

How does pollution affect the amount of light in an aquatic ecosystem?

1-3 Shine the flashlight through the cup of water. **Observe** and record how clear the water is and how much of the light shines through it. Use the dropper to add ten drops of milk to the water. Stir the mixture with a straw. Shine the flashlight through the cup of water again. **Observe** and record how clear the water is and how the light shines through it.

	Water Quality	How Much Light Shines Through?
Clear Water		
Milky Water		

Explain Your Results

1. How did the amount of light that traveled through the water differ in steps 1 and 3?

_____

2. What caused the difference?

_____

_____

3. Predict: What might happen to plants living in water if pollution caused the water to become cloudy?

_____

_____

_____

Self-Assessment Checklist

I **observed** and recorded how clear the water was and how the light shined through it. _____

I **observed** and recorded how clear the milky water was and how the light shined through it. _____

I described how the amount of light that traveled through the water differed in steps 1 and 3. _____

I explained what caused the difference. _____

I **predicted** what might happen to plants if pollution caused the water to become cloudy. _____

Notes for Home: Your child did an activity to **observe** how pollution affects the amount of light in an aquatic ecosystem.
Home Activity: With your child, discuss how pollution could affect plants on land.

Experiment: How does salt affect the hatching of brine shrimp?

Ask a question.

How does the amount of salt in the water affect how many brine shrimp eggs hatch?

State a hypothesis.

If brine shrimp eggs are put in water with no salt, a low salt level, a medium salt level, a high salt level, or a very high salt level, then in which will the most eggs hatch? Write your **hypothesis.**

_____

_____

Identify and control variables.

The amount of salt in the water is the **variable** that you will change. All the other conditions are **controlled.** They must be the same for all the cups.

Test your hypothesis.

❶–❹ Follow the steps to perform your experiment. Record your data in the chart.

Collect and record your data.

Cup	How many brine shrimp are moving? (none, a few, some, or many)			
	After 1 day	**After 2 days**	**After 3 days**	**After 4 days**
Cup A				
Cup B				
Cup C				
Cup D				
Cup E				

Interpret your data.

Analyze your data. Think about the salt level and how many brine shrimp were moving after 4 days. Use the chart on page 90 to help you rank the levels of salt based on how many shrimp were moving after 4 days.

Level of Salt (spoonfuls)

most ↑

Brine Shrimp Moving After 4 Days

↓ least

State your conclusion.
What conclusion can you draw from your data? Does it agree with your hypothesis? **Communicate** your conclusion.

_____

_____

_____

_____

_____

Go Further
How can you continue to observe the brine shrimp? Design and carry out a plan to extend the investigation or to answer this or other questions you may have.

_____

_____

_____

Self-Assessment Checklist	
I stated my **hypothesis** about how the amount of salt affects how many eggs hatch.	_____
I followed instructions to test my **hypothesis.**	_____
I **observed** the results and **collected data** in a chart.	_____
I **interpreted my data** by ranking the level of salt based on the number of moving shrimp.	_____
I **communicated** my conclusion.	_____

Notes for Home: Your child did an activity to determine how salt concentration affects the hatching of brine shrimp eggs.
Home Activity: Ask your child to explain to you how to set up an experiment that would test the effect of light on the hatching of brine shrimp.

Name _____

Explore: How can you make layers of water float on each other?

Explain Your Results

1. Infer: Suppose you weigh a spoonful of water from each layer. Which would be the heaviest? the lightest?

_____

_____

2. You observed the effect of salt and temperature together. How could you change the procedure to test only 1 variable, salt or temperature?

_____

_____

_____

_____

Self-Assessment Checklist	
I followed instructions to add the materials to the cups.	_____
I gently added drops of blue water and red water to the first cup.	_____
I **observed** that the layers of water floated on each other.	_____
I **made an inference** about the weights of equal volumes of the water from each layer.	_____
I explained how the procedure could be changed to test only 1 variable.	_____

Notes for Home: Your child did an activity to make layers of water of different densities float on each other.
Home Activity: With your child, make an **inference** about whether tap water floats on ocean water.

Activity Book

Investigate: What is a cloud?

4–5 Observe the bowls for 1 minute. Observe the bowls again after 5 and 10 minutes. Record your observations.

Time	Observations	
	Bowl With Warm Water	**Bowl Without Water**
After 1 minute		
After 5 minutes		
After 10 minutes		

Explain Your Results

1. Based on your **observations,** make an **inference.** Is there moisture in the air from which clouds form? Explain.

_____

_____

2. Use your **models** to describe some of the conditions necessary for clouds to form in the atmosphere.

_____

_____

_____

_____

_____

_____

Go Further

What effect does the ice have? Design and conduct a scientific investigation to answer this question or one of your own. Describe and demonstrate how to safely perform your investigation.

_____

_____

_____

_____

Self-Assessment Checklist	
I followed instructions to **make a model** to represent cloud formation.	_____
I **observed** the bowls for 1 minute and recorded my observations in the chart.	_____
I **observed** the bowls after 5 and 10 minutes and recorded my observations.	_____
I made an **inference** about the amount of moisture in the air from which clouds form.	_____
I used my **models** to describe some of the conditions necessary for clouds to form.	_____

Notes for Home: Your child did an activity to **observe** the role of moisture in cloud formation.
Home Activity: With your child, **observe** the clouds in the sky and discuss how they formed.

© Pearson Education, Inc.

Lab zone Activity

How does water pressure change as you go deeper in the ocean?

Materials

safety goggles

milk carton and water

nail

masking tape

pan

Process Skills

Think about the relationship between water depth and pressure as you make your **prediction.**

What to Do

1. Put on your safety goggles. Use the nail to punch three holes down the center of one side of the milk carton. The holes should all be the same size. Make one hole near the top of the carton, one in the middle, and one near the bottom.

   Be careful!
   Be careful when using the nail.

2. Cover the holes with a strip of masking tape.

3. Place the carton in the pan near one end. Be sure that the side of the carton with the holes is facing into the pan.

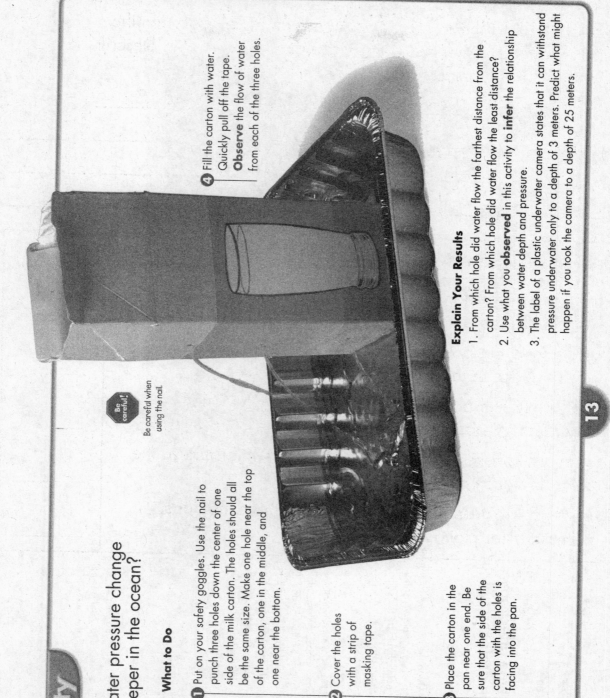

4. Fill the carton with water. Quickly pull off the tape. **Observe** the flow of water from each of the three holes.

Explain Your Results

1. From which hole did water flow the farthest distance from the carton? From which hole did water flow the least distance?

2. Use what you **observed** in this activity to **infer** the relationship between water depth and pressure.

3. The label of a plastic underwater camera states that it can withstand pressure underwater only to a depth of 3 meters. Predict what might happen if you took the camera to a depth of 25 meters.

13

Name _____

Activity

How does soil type affect how much water can drain through it?

Materials

safety goggles

nail

4 cups

newspaper

sand and soil

water and measuring cup

clock

Process Skills

You can make a prediction based on your observations.

What to Do

1. Using the nail, poke four holes in the bottoms of two of the cups. The holes should be the same size in each cup.

2. Place the cups with holes on the newspaper. Fill one cup three-quarters full with sand. Fill the second cup three-quarters full with soil. Press down lightly on the soil. Make sure that both cups are filled to the same height.

Be careful!

Be careful when punching holes with the nail.

3. Place the cup with the sand inside another cup. Pour one-half cup of water into the cup with the sand.

4. Allow the water to drain through the sand for 3 minutes. **Observe** how much water drains through the sand into the empty cup.

5. Repeat steps 3 and 4 using the cup filled with soil.

Explain Your Results

1. Which of the cups had more water drain through it? Why do you think this happened?

2. **Predict** Which type of soil will absorb more water during a heavy rainstorm—an area covered with soil or a sandy beach?

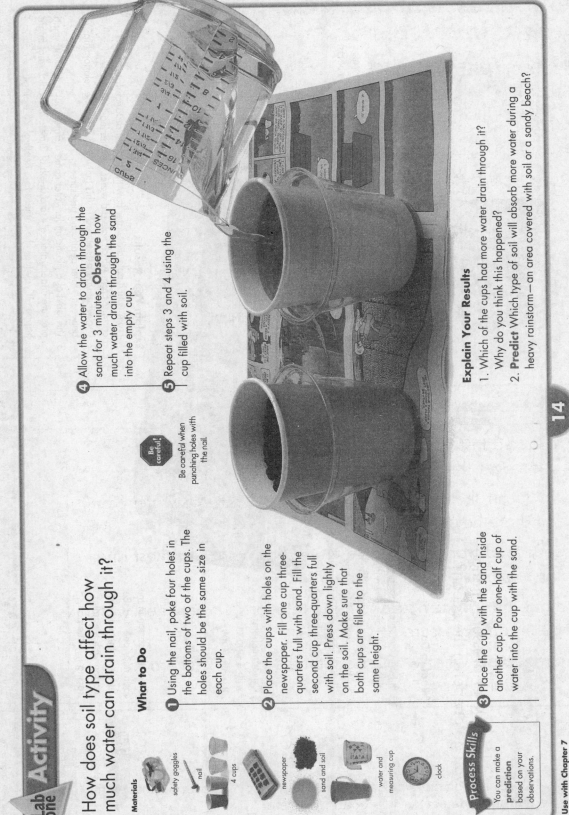

14

How does water pressure change as you go deeper in the ocean?

Explain Your Results

1. From which hole did water flow the farthest distance from the carton? From which hole did water flow the least distance?

_____

2. Use what you **observed** in this activity to **infer** the relationship between water depth and pressure.

_____

3. The label of a plastic underwater camera states that it can withstand pressure underwater only to a depth of 3 meters. **Predict** what might happen if you took the camera to a depth of 25 meters.

_____

Self-Assessment Checklist	
I followed instructions to punch three holes in the carton and cover them with tape.	_____
I pulled off the tape and **observed** the flow of water from the three holes.	_____
I described from which hole water flowed the farthest and the least distance from the carton.	_____
I made an **inference** about the relationship between water depth and pressure.	_____
I **predicted** what would happen if I took a camera to 25 meters.	_____

Notes for Home: Your child did an activity to **observe** how water pressure changes the deeper you go in the ocean.
Home Activity: With your child, discuss how pressure in the ocean affects where certain organisms can live.

How does soil type affect how much water can drain through it?

Explain Your Results

1. Which of the cups had more water drain through it? Why do you think this happened?

_____

2. Predict: Which type of soil will absorb more water during a heavy rainstorm—an area covered with soil or a sandy beach?

_____

Self-Assessment Checklist	
I followed instructions to poke 4 holes in the bottoms of 2 of the large cups.	_____
I followed instructions to fill the cups with sand or soil and allowed water to drain through them.	_____
I **observed** how much water drained through the two types of soil.	_____
I explained which of the cups had more water drain through it and why this happened.	_____
I **predicted** which type of soil would absorb more water during a heavy rainstorm.	_____

Notes for Home: Your child did an activity to **observe** how different types of soil absorb different amounts of water.
Home Activity: With your child, **observe** how the soil in your neighborhood absorbs water and compare it to the soil studied in class.

Use with Chapter 8, p. 228

Explore: How does pressure affect an object?

4 **Observe** the target on the marshmallow for any small changes in size. Write your **observations**.

_____

_____

_____

Explain Your Results

1. How did the marshmallow change when the pressure was increased and decreased?

_____

_____

_____

2. Infer: Why did the size of the marshmallow change when the pressure increased?

_____

_____

_____

_____

_____

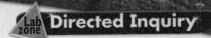
Self-Assessment Checklist	
I followed instructions to prepare a marshmallow and put it inside a jar sealed with clay.	_____
I followed instructions to change the air pressure by sucking and then blowing.	_____
I **observed** the marshmallow for changes in size.	_____
I described how the marshmallow changed when the pressure was increased and decreased.	_____
I made an **inference** about why the size changed when the pressure increased.	_____

Notes for Home: Your child did an activity to observe the effects of air pressure.
Home Activity: With your child, use your knowledge of air pressure to make an inference about why air rushes out of a 2-liter soda bottle when you open it.

Investigate: How does a thermometer work?

4 Place the thermometer in warm water. **Observe** whether the red liquid in the straw moves higher, moves lower, or does not change.

5 **Predict** whether the red liquid in the straw will move higher or lower when you place the thermometer in cold water. Record your **prediction.** Record your **observation.**

Thermometer in Warm Water	Thermometer in Cold Water	
Observation	Prediction	Observation

Explain Your Results

1. What evidence did you use to make your **prediction?**

_____

_____

2. Explain how you think your thermometer works.

_____

_____

_____

_____

Go Further

How could you use weather instruments to describe weather patterns and how weather changes? Collect and analyze weather data.

_____

_____

Self-Assessment Checklist	
I followed instructions to make a thermometer.	_____
I **observed** the movement of the liquid in the thermometer.	_____
I recorded my **prediction** and **observations** in the chart.	_____
I described the evidence I used to help make my **prediction**.	_____
I explained how I think my thermometer works.	

© Pearson Education, Inc.

Notes for Home: Your child did an activity to make a thermometer.
Home Activity: With your child, observe the outside temperature for a week.

Lab zone Activity

How does the amount of sunlight reaching Earth vary at different places?

Materials

globe

clay

2 thermometers

lamp

metric ruler

clock

Process Skills

Making a model can help you **infer** how solar radiation affects temperatures at different locations on Earth.

What to Do

1 Separate the clay into two lumps. Push one thermometer onto a piece of clay as shown in the picture. Do the same with the second thermometer and another piece of clay.

2 Choose two places on one side of the globe. One place should be near the equator. The other place should be near a polar region. Stick the clay pieces on the globe at your chosen places.

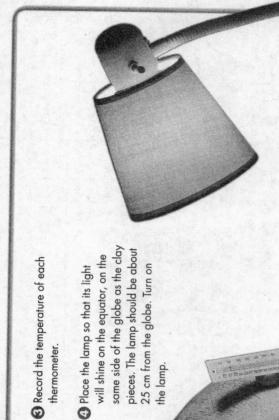

3 Record the temperature of each thermometer.

4 Place the lamp so that its light will shine on the equator, on the same side of the globe as the clay pieces. The lamp should be about 25 cm from the globe. Turn on the lamp.

5 After 15 minutes, turn off the lamp. Record the temperature on each of the thermometers.

Explain Your Results

1. **Observe** How did the temperatures of the thermometers differ in steps 3 and 5?

2. Which place had the higher temperature in step 5? Why do you think this is so?

3. What does the lamp represent in the **model?** Use the model to explain why some areas of Earth get more sunlight than others.

15

Lab zone Activity

How does a barometer work?

Materials

scissors and tape

balloon and rubber band

jar

toothpicks

paper

metric ruler and straw

What to Do

1. Use the scissors to cut off the neck of the balloon. Stretch the balloon over the opening of the jar. Place the rubber band around the neck of the jar to hold the balloon in place.

2. Tape the toothpick to one end of the straw. Tape the other end of the straw to the center of the balloon covering the jar opening.

3. At the top of the piece of paper, draw a Sun. Use the metric ruler to draw marks down the sheet of paper beneath the Sun. The marks should be 1 cm apart. Number the marks, beginning at the bottom. At the bottom of the paper beneath the marks, draw clouds and rain.

4. Place your barometer on a table near a wall. Tape the sheet of paper to the wall behind the barometer. The toothpick should be even with the center mark.

5. Lightly push down on the balloon. Observe what happens to the toothpick.

6. For the next few days, observe and record where the toothpick is pointing. Make your observations several times each day. Also record the weather at the time you take each reading.

Explain Your Results

1. How did your barometer reading change throughout the day? From day to day?

2. **Infer** What causes the toothpick on your barometer to move up and down?

3. Did the weather change when the reading on the barometer changed? How?

Process Skills

You can make a barometer and infer how it works.

How does the amount of sunlight reaching Earth vary at different places?

3 Record the temperature of each thermometer.

	Temperature of Thermometer	
	Equator	**Polar Region**
Start		
15 minutes		

5 After 15 minutes, turn off the lamp. Record the temperature on each of the thermometers.

Explain Your Results

1. Observe: How did the temperatures of the thermometers differ in steps 3 and 5?

_____

_____

2. Which place had the higher temperature in step 5? Why do you think this is so?

_____

_____

3. What does the lamp represent in the **model?** Use the model to explain why some areas of Earth get more sunlight than others.

_____

_____

_____

Self-Assessment Checklist	
I followed instructions to stick the thermometers to the globe and recorded the temperature.	_____
I shined light on the globe and recorded the temperature again after 15 minutes.	_____
I **observed** how the temperatures of the thermometers differed in steps 4 and 5.	_____
I explained which place had the higher temperature in step 5.	_____
I used the **model** to explain why some areas of Earth get more sunlight than others.	_____

Notes for Home: Your child did an activity to **observe** how the amount of sunlight reaching Earth varies at different places.
Home Activity: With your child, discuss what other factors affect the temperature of a region.

© Pearson Education, Inc.

How does a barometer work?

5 Lightly push down on the balloon. **Observe** what happens to the toothpick.

_____

6 For the next few days, observe and record where the toothpick is pointing. Make your observations several times each day. Also record the weather at the time you take each reading.

Date and Time	Observation	Weather Outside

Explain Your Results

1. How did your barometer reading change throughout the day? From day to day?

_____

_____

2. Infer: What causes the toothpick on your barometer to move up and down?

_____

3. Did the weather change when the reading on the barometer changed? How?

_____

_____

Self-Assessment Checklist	
I followed instructions to make a barometer.	_____
I **observed** and recorded where the toothpick was pointing and the weather.	_____
I described how my barometer reading changed from day to day and throughout the day.	_____
I made an **inference** about what caused the toothpick on my barometer to move up and down.	_____
I explained how the weather changed when the reading on the barometer changed.	_____

Notes for Home: Your child did an activity to make a barometer and **observe** how it works.
Home Activity: With your child, **observe** a weather map showing different areas of barometric pressure.

Explore: How can you make a model of material found deep in Earth?

2 Pour the mixture into your hand. Does it have the properties of a liquid or a solid? Record your **observations.**

_____

_____

3 Close your hand and squeeze. How do the mixture's properties seem to change?

_____

_____

Explain Your Results

Do you think the mixture acts like both a solid and a liquid? **Communicate** your reasons.

_____

_____

Self-Assessment Checklist	
I followed instructions to combine cornstarch and water in a cup.	
I **poured** the mixture into my hands.	_____
I told whether the mixture in my hands had the properties of a liquid or a solid.	
I **observed** how the mixture's properties change when I squeeze it.	_____
I **communicated** my reasons for why the mixture acts like both a liquid and a solid.	_____

Notes for Home: Your child did an activity to **infer** the properties of Earth's mantle.
Home Activity: With your child, discuss how ordinary liquids, like water, can turn into solids.

Investigate: What buildings are less damaged by an earthquake?

1 Ask questions about what helps a building survive an earthquake. Record your questions here.

_____

_____

_____

3 Test your buildings. Record your results. Repeat your test 2 more times.

Describe or Draw Building	Results (toppled 1st, toppled 2nd, toppled 3rd, or toppled 4th)			Overall Results (best, 2nd best, 3rd best, worst)
	Trial 1	**Trial 2**	**Trial 3**	
Building A				
Building B				
Building C				
Building D				

Explain Your Results

1. Describe the device and procedure you used to test your buildings. Why did you repeat your test?

_____

_____

_____

_____

2. How were you limited in what you could build?

_____

_____

3. Look at the data in the chart. Look for patterns. Think about your **models.** What features might help a building to survive an earthquake?

_____

_____

Go Further

Replace the sugar cubes with buildings made of marshmallows connected with toothpicks. Are the results similar? Make a plan and change your model to answer this question or one of your own.

_____

Self-Assessment Checklist	
I asked questions about what helps a building survive an earthquake.	_____
I designed and built 4 different **models** of buildings.	_____
I tested my buildings and recorded the results.	_____
I described the test of my buildings and explained why I repeated the test.	_____
I described limits on what could be built.	_____
I interpreted data to determine what features might help a building to survive an earthquake. I discussed my ideas with others.	_____

Notes for Home: Your child designed an experiment to investigate what buildings are least damaged by earthquakes.
Home Activity: With your child, research the history of earthquakes in your region.

Name _____

© Pearson Education, Inc.

Lab zone Activity

How does water erode soil?

Materials

shoe box

scissors and metric ruler

soil

dropper

water

What to Do

1 Set up the activity as shown.

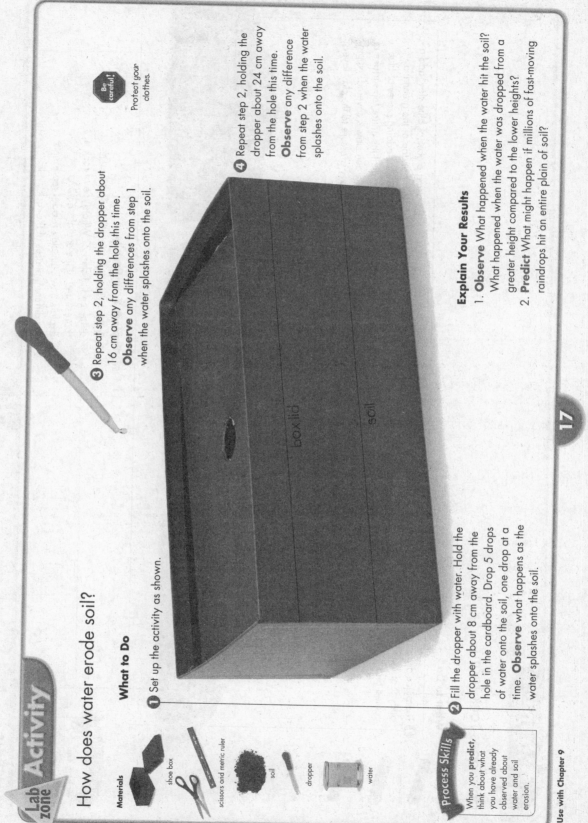

soil

box lid

2 Fill the dropper with water. Hold the dropper about 8 cm away from the hole in the cardboard. Drop 5 drops of water onto the soil, one drop at a time. **Observe** what happens as the water splashes onto the soil.

3 Repeat step 2, holding the dropper about 16 cm away from the hole this time. **Observe** any differences from step 1 when the water splashes onto the soil.

4 Repeat step 2, holding the dropper about 24 cm away from the hole this time. **Observe** any difference from step 2 when the water splashes onto the soil.

Be careful!

Protect your clothes.

Explain Your Results

1. **Observe** What happened when the water hit the soil? What happened when the water was dropped from a greater height compared to the lower heights?

2. **Predict** What might happen if millions of fast-moving raindrops hit an entire plain of soil?

Activity Book

Lab zone Activity

How does rock form?

Materials

red modeling clay

green modeling clay

blue modeling clay

What to Do

1. The piece of red clay represents a layer of igneous rock that has cooled and hardened.

2. Using pieces of green clay, add a layer on top of the red clay. Continue adding pieces of green clay until the entire top surface of the red clay is covered. Apply a moderate amount of pressure to the clay layers.

3. Using pieces of blue clay, add a layer on top of the green clay. Continue adding pieces of blue clay until the entire top surface of the green clay is covered. Apply heavy pressure to the clay layers.

Explain Your Results

1. **Infer** What type of rock is represented at the end of step 2? What type of rock is represented at the end of step 3?

2. Explain how your clay **model** represents the different phases of the rock cycle.

Process Skills

Making and using **models** can help you **infer** how something works.

18

How does water erode soil?

②–④ Fill the dropper with water. Hold the dropper about 8 cm away from the hole in the cardboard. Drop 5 drops of water onto the soil, one drop at a time. **Observe** what happens as the water splashes onto the soil. Repeat step 2, holding the dropper about 16 cm away from the hole this time. **Observe** any differences from step 2 when the water splashes onto the soil. Repeat step 2, holding the dropper about 24 cm away from the hole this time. **Observe** any difference from step 2 when the water splashes onto the soil.

Height	Observations
8 cm	
16 cm	
24 cm	

Explain Your Results

1. Observe: What happened when the water hit the soil? What happened when the water was dropped from a greater height compared to the lower heights?

_____

_____

_____

2. Predict: What might happen if millions of fast-moving raindrops hit an entire plain of soil?

_____

Self-Assessment Checklist

I followed instructions to set up the activity as shown.   _____

I followed instructions to fill the dropper with water.   _____

I dropped water onto the soil from different heights and
observed what happened each time.   _____

I explained what happened when the water was dropped
from a greater height.   _____

I **predicted** what might happen if millions of fast-moving
raindrops hit an entire plain of soil.   _____

Notes for Home: Your child did an activity to **observe** how water erodes soil.
Home Activity: With your child, discuss what might happen to the animals living
on the plain that experienced erosion in the activity.

Activity Book

How does rock form?

Explain Your Results

1. **Infer:** What type of rock is represented at the end of step 2? What type of rock is represented at the end of step 3?

_____

2. Explain how your clay **model** represents the different phases of the rock cycle.

_____

_____

_____

_____

_____

_____

Self-Assessment Checklist	
I added a layer of green clay until the entire top surface of the red clay was covered.	
I applied a moderate amount of pressure to the clay layers.	____
I added a layer of blue clay on top of the green clay and applied heavy pressure.	____
I **classified** the rock represented at the end of steps 2 and 3.	____
I explained how my clay **model** represents the different phases of the rock cycle.	____

Notes for Home: Your child did an activity to **make a model** of how rock forms. **Home Activity:** With your child, discuss the process by which rock changes to sand.

Explore: How does oil rise through the Earth?

3 Wait 5 minutes. Can you see any droplets of oil? Use a hand lens. Can you smell oil on the sponge? Take off a glove. Touch the top of the sponge. Does it feel oily?

_____

Explain Your Results

1. In your **model,** how did the oil get to the surface?

_____

2. Infer: Often, as oil rises, it becomes trapped in different places deep underground. How do you think people get this oil?

_____

_____

Self-Assessment Checklist	
I followed instructions to put the sponge in the cup of oil and squeeze the sponge.	
I followed instructions to place the sponge in the cup with warm water.	_____
I waited 5 minutes and examined the sponge for droplets of oil and for an oily smell and feel.	_____
I explained how the oil got to the surface in my **model.**	_____
I made an **inference** about how people get oil that is trapped in different places deep underground.	_____

Notes for Home: Your child did an activity to **make a model** of how oil rises through the Earth.
Home Activity: With your child, discuss how oil is formed in the ground.

Investigate: How can paper be recycled?

6 **Collect Data:** Compare your recycled paper to newspaper. Record their properties.

Kind of Paper	Properties
Newspaper	
Recycled paper	

Explain Your Results

1. Interpret Data: How was your recycled paper like the paper with which you started? How was it different?

_____

_____

2. What natural resource did you conserve by recycling paper?

_____

_____

Go Further

How can you collect and classify different recyclable materials? How can renewable resources be maintained? Make a plan to find out.

_____

_____

_____

_____

Guided Inquiry

Self-Assessment Checklist	
I followed instructions to prepare the newspaper and leave it in the bowl of water for 1 hour.	_____
I followed instructions to make paper mush and spread it on the screen to make recycled paper.	_____
I **collected data** about and compared the properties of the newspaper and the recycled paper.	_____
I **interpreted** my **data** to describe how the two kinds of paper were alike and different.	_____
I named the natural resource conserved by recycling paper.	_____

Notes for Home: Your child did an activity to make recycled paper from newspaper.
Home Activity: With your child, discuss what household objects you can recycle in your community.

Name _____

Lab zone **Activity**

How does an oil spill spread?

Materials

1 large pan

water

1 toothpick

oil

metric ruler

stopwatch

What to Do

1. Fill the pan three-quarters full with tap water.

2. Place the tip of the toothpick in the oil. Remove the toothpick from the oil. Let the excess oil drip off the end of the toothpick back into the container of oil.

3. Place the tip of the toothpick in the center of the pan of water. Remove it quickly.

Be careful!
Protect your clothes.

4. Begin timing as soon as the toothpick touches the water. Time for 30 seconds. After 30 seconds, use the ruler to measure the diameter of the oil spread.

5. Repeat step 4 every 30 seconds for 2 minutes.

6. Collect data about what you observe.

Explain Your Results

1. **Interpret Data** What happened to the diameter of the oil spill as time passed?

2. **Infer** Explain why oil spills are hard to contain and clean up when they occur in oceans.

Process Skills

You make an inference when you interpret data you collect.

Use with Chapter 10

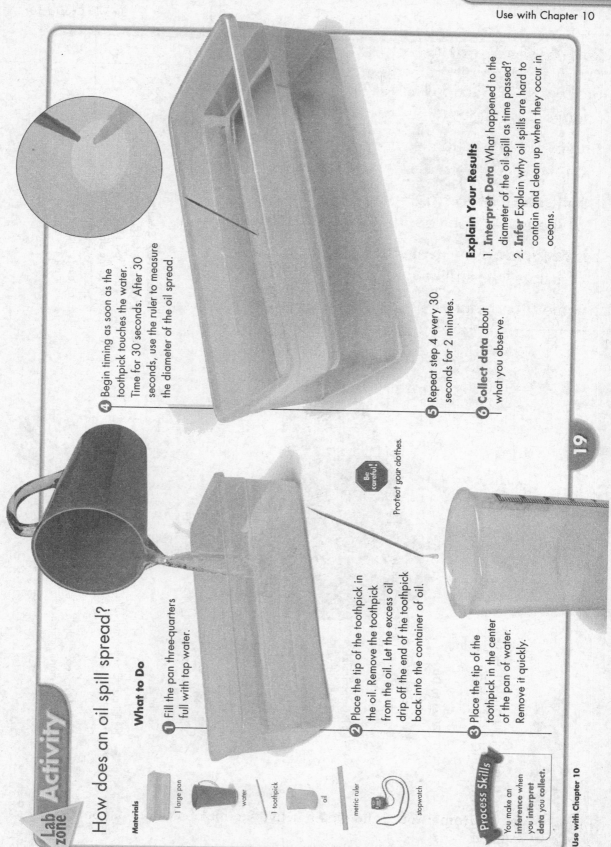

19

How does an oil spill spread?

4–6 Begin timing as soon as the toothpick touches the water. Time for 30 seconds. After 30 seconds, use the ruler to measure the diameter of the oil spread. Repeat step 4 every 30 seconds for 2 minutes. **Collect data** about what you observe.

Time (sec)	30	60	90	120
Diameter (cm)				

Explain Your Results

1. Interpret Data: What happened to the diameter of the oil spill as time passed?

_____

2. Infer: Explain why oil spills are hard to contain and clean up when they occur in oceans.

_____

_____

_____

Self-Assessment Checklist	
I followed instructions to place the toothpick in the oil and then in the center of the pan.	_____
I used the ruler to measure the diameter of the oil spread every 30 seconds.	_____
I **collected data** about what I observed.	_____
I **interpreted my data** to explain what happened to the diameter of the oil spill as time passed.	_____
I made an **inference** about why oil spills are hard to contain and clean up.	_____

Notes for Home: Your child did an activity to **observe** how an oil spill spreads.
Home Activity: With your child, discuss what effect oil spills have on the environment.

How does acid rain affect buildings and statues?

6 Allow the cups to sit for 15 minutes. After 15 minutes **observe** what changes have taken place in the cups.

	Observations
Cup 1	
Cup 2	
Cup 3	
Cup 4	

Explain Your Results

1. Observe: What happened in each of the cups? How does this experiment model the effects of acid rain?

_____

_____

_____

_____

_____

2. Infer: How might acid rain affect buildings and statues?

_____

© Pearson Education, Inc.

Self-Assessment Checklist

I followed instructions to fill cups 1 and 2 with water and cups 3 and 4 with vinegar.

     _____

I followed instructions to put pieces of chalk and marble chips in the cups.

     _____

I **observed** the changes that took place in the cups after 15 minutes.

     _____

I explained how this experiment models the effects of acid rain.

     _____

I made an **inference** about how acid rain might affect buildings and statues.

     _____

Notes for Home: Your child did an activity to **observe** how acid rain affects buildings and statues.
Home Activity: With your child, see if you can find a statue or a building in your town that has been affected by acid rain.

Name _____

Experiment: How does temperature affect the growth of crystals?

Ask a question.

How does the temperature at which crystals form affect their size?

State a hypothesis.

If crystals form at a higher temperature, then will they be larger, smaller, or about the same size as crystals formed at a lower temperature? Write your **hypothesis.**

_____

_____

_____

Identify and control variables.

Temperature is the independent variable, the thing you will change. Crystal size is the dependent variable, the thing that is affected by the temperature change. The amount of salol you will use is a **controlled variable,** something that must not change.

Test your hypothesis.

❶–❹ Follow the steps to perform your experiment. Record your data in the chart.

Collect and record your data.

| | Size and Appearance of Crystals ||
	Crystals Formed at Room Temperature	**Crystals Formed at Cold Temperature**
Drawing or Sketch		
Description		

© Pearson Education, Inc.

Interpret your data.

Compare the size of the crystals formed at room temperature with the size of the crystals formed at a cold temperature.

_____

_____

State your conclusion.

Explain how the temperature at which crystals form affects their size. Compare your hypothesis with your results. **Communicate** your conclusion.

_____

_____

Go Further

What would happen if you did not add any grains of salol to the melted salol? Would the formation of crystals be affected? Design and carry out a plan to investigate this or other questions you may have.

_____

_____

_____

Self-Assessment Checklist	
I stated my **hypothesis** about how the temperature at which crystals form affects their size.	_____
I followed instructions to test my **hypothesis** and **observed** the results.	_____
I **collected data** about the size and appearance of the crystals in a chart.	_____
I compared the size of the crystals formed at the two different temperatures.	_____
I **communicated** my conclusion.	_____

 Notes for Home: Your child conducted an experiment to determine how the temperature at which crystals form affects their size.
Home Activity: With your child, find another example of a crystal, such as sugar, and **observe** it under a hand lens or another magnifying device.

Explore: What is one way you can determine density?

❶ **Measure** the length, width, and height of a wooden block in centimeters. Find the block's volume in cubic centimeters.

_____ × _____ × _____ = _____
   length   width   height   volume

❷ Use a balance to measure the mass of the block.

mass of the block is: _____

❸ Calculate the block's density.

_____ ÷ _____ = _____
   mass   volume   density

❹ Repeat steps 1–3 with $\frac{1}{4}$ of a stick of clay, $\frac{1}{2}$ of a stick of clay, and a gram cube. Record your data in the chart on page 134.

$\frac{1}{4}$ **stick of clay** _____ × _____ × _____ = _____
                length   width   height   volume

_____ ÷ _____ = _____
     mass   volume   density

$\frac{1}{2}$ **stick of clay** _____ × _____ × _____ = _____
                length   width   height   volume

_____ ÷ _____ = _____
     mass   volume   density

gram cube _____ × _____ × _____ = _____
                length   width   height   volume

_____ ÷ _____ = _____
     mass   volume   density

Object	Volume	Density
wooden block		
$\frac{1}{4}$ stick of clay		
$\frac{1}{2}$ stick of clay		
gram cube		

Explain Your Results

Communicate: Describe one way to find the density of an object. What must you **measure?**

_____

_____

_____

Self-Assessment Checklist	
I followed instructions to find the volume, mass, and density of a wooden block.	_____
I followed instructions to find the volume, mass, and density of $\frac{1}{4}$ stick of clay.	_____
I followed instructions to find the volume, mass, and density of $\frac{1}{2}$ stick of clay.	_____
I followed instructions to find the volume, mass, and density of a gram cube.	_____
I **communicated** how to find the density of an object.	_____

Notes for Home: Your child did an activity to determine how the volume, mass, and density of solids can be measured and compared.
Home Activity: Have your child explain to you how to find the density of a piece of chalk.

Investigate: What boat design will carry the most cargo?

❶ Design a boat that will support the most cargo. Explain why you picked your design solution. Identify which materials will work best for your design. Make a plan or a procedure. _____

_____

_____

❷ Construct your **model** boat. Measure its length, width, and height in cm. Record your measurements in the chart.

❸ Test your boat design. **Predict** how many pennies your boat will hold. Record your prediction in the chart. Add cargo (pennies) to your boat. Record the number of pennies you add before your boat sinks.

❹ Use a balance to **measure** the mass of the cargo in grams. Record the mass.

Test Results				
Size of Boat (cm)	**List of Materials Used**	**Amount of Cargo Carried Without Sinking** (number of pennies)		**Mass of Cargo** (grams)
		Predicted	**Observed**	
length _____ cm width _____ cm height _____ cm		_____	_____	_____

Explain Your Results

1. Sketch your model boat design. Explain what caused your boat to sink.

_____

_____

_____

2. Interpret Data: Evaluate your model boat design. Was it more or less successful than the designs of the other groups? Explain.

_____

_____

3. What shape, size, and material made the boat that could carry the most cargo?

_____

_____

Go Further

Review your procedure and design with other students. Compare and contrast your investigation with theirs. Ask yourself and the other students questions about how your design could be improved. Use their comments to help you make your revisions.

_____

_____

_____

Self-Assessment Checklist	
I followed instructions to construct a **model** boat.	_____
I tested my boat design by determining how many pennies it would hold.	_____
I **recorded data** in the chart.	_____
I sketched my boat design and explained why it sank.	_____
I evaluated my design and determined the boat properties that supported the most cargo.	_____

Notes for Home: Your child applied knowledge of density to build a **model** boat with the most capacity possible.
Home Activity: With your child, research boats on the Internet and compare them to the one constructed in class.

© Pearson Education, Inc.

Lab zone Activity

Do water molecules have any space between them?

Materials

plastic cup

paper plate

water

paper towels

teaspoon

salt

What to Do

1 Set the cup in the middle of the paper plate. Fill the cup to the top with water. Continue to add water slowly until the cup begins to overflow, then stop.

2 Carefully soak up the water on the plate using the paper towels. It is important not to move the cup or the plate as you do this.

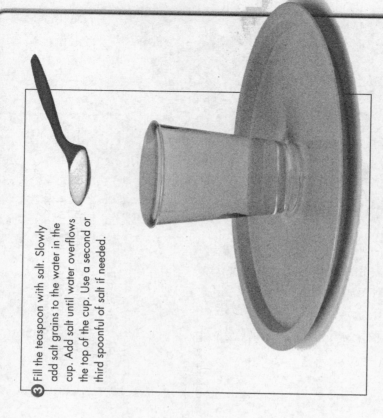

3 Fill the teaspoon with salt. Slowly add salt grains to the water in the cup. Add salt until water overflows the top of the cup. Use a second or third spoonful of salt if needed.

Explain Your Results

1. **Observe** How much salt were you able to add to the water? How is this possible if the cup was already full?

2. **Infer** What would happen if you had added a marble to the already full cup of water instead of the salt?

Process Skills

You can make an inference based on what you observe during an experiment.

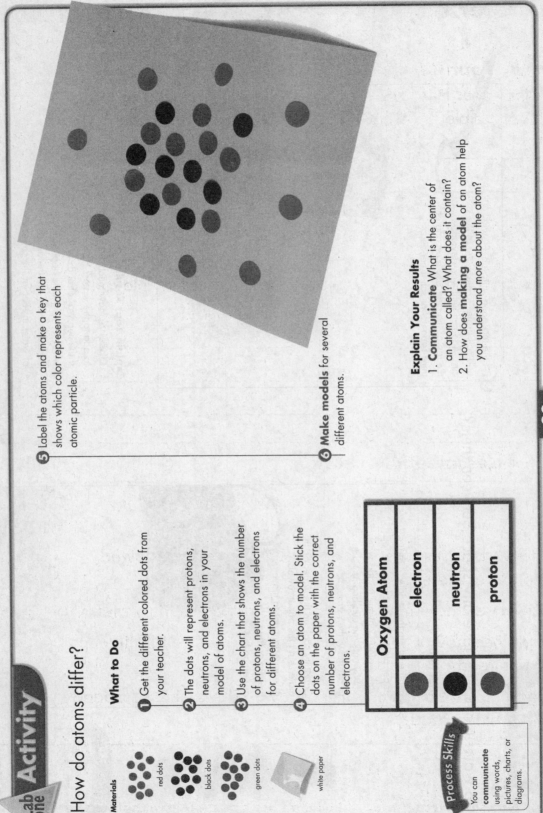

Lab Activity zone

How do atoms differ?

Materials

red dots

black dots

green dots

white paper

What to Do

1. Get the different colored dots from your teacher.

2. The dots will represent protons, neutrons, and electrons in your model of atoms.

3. Use the chart that shows the number of protons, neutrons, and electrons for different atoms.

4. Choose an atom to model. Stick the dots on the paper with the correct number of protons, neutrons, and electrons.

5. Label the atoms and make a key that shows which color represents each atomic particle.

6. **Make models** for several different atoms.

Oxygen Atom	
electron	●
neutron	●
proton	●

Process Skills

You can **communicate** using words, pictures, charts, or diagrams.

Explain Your Results

1. **Communicate** What is the center of an atom called? What does it contain?

2. How does **making a model** of an atom help you understand more about the atom?

Do water molecules have any space between them?

Explain Your Results

1. Observe: How much salt were you able to add to the water? How is this possible if the cup was already full?

_____

_____

_____

_____

2. Infer: What would happen if you added a marble to the already full cup of water instead of the salt?

_____

_____

_____

Self-Assessment Checklist	
I followed instructions to fill the cup with water until it overflowed.	_____
I followed instructions to add salt until water overflowed the top of the cup.	_____
I **observed** how much salt could be added to the water.	_____
I explained how it was possible to add more salt if the cup was already full.	_____
I made an **inference** about what would happen if I added a marble instead.	_____

 Notes for Home: Your child did an activity to **observe** that water molecules have space.
Home Activity: With your child, discuss whether or not air has mass.

How do atoms differ?

Explain Your Results

1. Communicate: What is the center of an atom called? What does it contain?

_____

_____

2. How does **making a model** of an atom help you understand more about the atom?

_____

_____

_____

Self-Assessment Checklist	
I **made models** for several different atoms on the paper using the dots.	_____
I used the chart that showed the number of protons, neutrons, and electrons for different atoms.	_____
I labeled the atoms and made a key that showed which color represents each atomic particle.	_____
I **communicated** what the center of the atom is called and what it contains.	_____
I described how **making a model** of an atom helps explain more about the atom.	_____

Notes for Home: Your child did an activity to **make a model** of an atom.
Home Activity: Have your child explain to you what an electron is.

Explore: What can happen during a chemical change?

①–④ Follow instructions to add chemicals to the water. Record the temperatures in the chart.

Cup	Contents of Cup	Temperature (after 1 minute) (°C)
Cup A	Water	
	Water and Alka-Seltzer® tablets	
Cup B	Water	
	Water, baking soda, and calcium chloride	

Explain Your Results

Use the **data** you **collected** to make an **inference.** In which reaction was energy lost?

_____

Self-Assessment Checklist	
I followed instructions to prepare the cups.	_____
I **measured** the temperature of the water in cup A before and after adding the tablets.	_____
I **measured** the temperature of the water in cup B before and after adding the chemicals.	_____
I recorded my measurements in the chart.	_____
I **inferred** in which reaction energy was lost.	_____

Notes for Home: Your child did an activity to observe what can happen during a chemical change.
Home Activity: With your child, discuss other chemical reactions that are common around the home.

Name _____

Investigate: How does temperature affect how long a reaction takes?

①–③ Measure and record the number of seconds required to complete the chemical reaction. Repeat with room temperature water and warm water. Make a chart to help **collect** your **data.**

Trial	Water Temperature (°C)	Time (seconds)
Ice-cold water		
Room-temperature water		
Warm water		

Explain Your Results

1. Report the **data** you **collected.** Think of a way to show the times required to complete the chemical reactions. You could make a bar graph (like the one below), a line graph, or a diagram. You may select a different way to report the data.

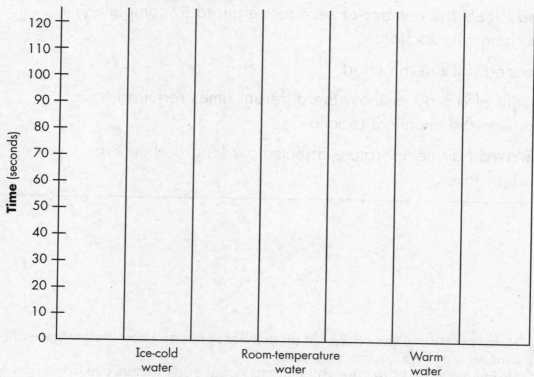

2. Infer: How does temperature affect how long a chemical reaction takes?

_____

_____

Go Further

If you repeat the activity several times, will you get similar results? With your teacher's permission, make and carry out a plan to find out. When finished, give an oral report to your class.

_____

_____

_____

_____

Self-Assessment Checklist	
I followed instructions to add Alka-Seltzer® tablets to water of different temperatures.	_____
I **measured** the number of seconds required to complete the chemical reaction.	_____
I recorded data in the chart.	_____
I thought of a way to show the different times required to complete the chemical reaction.	_____
I **inferred** how temperature affects how long a chemical reaction takes.	_____

Notes for Home: Your child did an activity to observe how temperature affects how long a chemical reaction takes.
Home Activity: With your child, discuss what other factors can affect how long a chemical reaction takes.

Activity Book

© Pearson Education, Inc.

Lab zone Activity

What can speed up a chemical reaction?

Materials

4 plastic cups

water

pieces of effervescent tablets

paper towels

metal spoon

Process Skills

When you make a prediction, you state what you expect the results to be.

What to Do

1 Fill one cup halfway with cold water. Fill a second cup halfway with very warm water. It is important that both cups have the same amount of water.

2 Place half of an effervescent tablet in each cup at exactly the same time. **Observe** the rate at which each tablet fizzes and dissolves.

Be careful!

Do not drink the effervescent tablet solution.

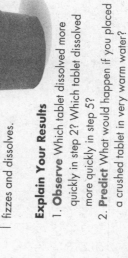

3 Place half of an effervescent tablet in the third cup. Use the spoon to crush the tablet into a powder.

4 Place half of an effervescent tablet in the fourth cup.

5 Fill each cup half full with room-temperature water. **Observe** the rate at which each tablet fizzes and dissolves.

Explain Your Results

1. **Observe** Which tablet dissolved more quickly in step 2? Which tablet dissolved more quickly in step 5?

2. **Predict** What would happen if you placed a crushed tablet in very warm water?

23

Lab Zone Activity

How can you observe evidence of a chemical change?

Materials

3 cups

2 thermometers

steel wool pad

scissors and masking tape

vinegar

plastic wrap

clock

What to Do

1. Label two of the cups A and B using the masking tape. Put the thermometers in two of the cups. Record the temperatures.

2. Cut two pieces of steel wool. Wrap one piece around the thermometer from cup A. Put the other piece in the empty cup and cover it with vinegar. Let it soak for one minute.

3. Squeeze the vinegar out of the steel wool and wrap it around the thermometer from cup B. Cover both cups with plastic wrap.

4. Record the temperature every 2 minutes for 10 minutes. **Observe** what happens to the steel wool.

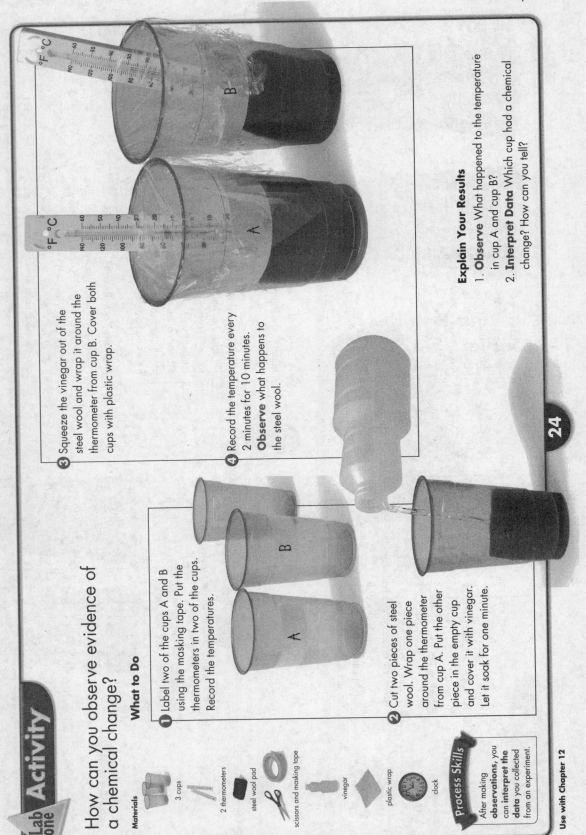

Explain Your Results

1. **Observe** What happened to the temperature in cup A and cup B?

2. **Interpret Data** Which cup had a chemical change? How can you tell?

Process Skills

After making **observations**, you can **interpret the data** you collected from an experiment.

24

What can speed up a chemical reaction?

❶–❷ Fill one cup halfway with cold water. Fill a second cup halfway with very warm water. Place half of an effervescent tablet in each cup at exactly the same time. **Observe** the rate at which each tablet fizzes and dissolves.

_____

❸–❺ Place half of an effervescent tablet in the third cup. Use the spoon to crush the tablet into a powder. Place half of an effervescent tablet in the fourth cup. Fill each cup half full with room-temperature water. **Observe** the rate at which each tablet fizzes and dissolves.

_____

Explain Your Results

1. Observe: Which tablet dissolved more quickly in step 2? Which tablet dissolved more quickly in step 5?

_____

_____

_____

2. Predict: What would happen if you placed a crushed tablet in very warm water?

_____

_____

Self-Assessment Checklist	
I followed instructions to fill each cup halfway with water.	_____
I **observed** the rate at which each tablet fizzed and dissolved.	_____
I followed instructions to place a crushed tablet in one cup and an uncrushed tablet in another cup.	_____
I again **observed** the rate at which each tablet fizzed and dissolved.	_____
I **predicted** what would happen if I placed a crushed tablet in hot water.	_____

Notes for Home: Your child did an activity to **observe** factors that can speed up a chemical reaction.
Home Activity: With your child, discuss why an organism's body might intentionally slow down or speed up a chemical reaction.

How can you observe evidence of a chemical change?

1-4 Label two of the cups cup A and cup B using the masking tape. Put thermometers in cups A and B. Record the temperatures in the chart below. Cut two pieces of steel wool. Wrap one piece around the thermometer from cup A. Put the other piece in the empty cup and cover it with vinegar. Let it soak for 1 minute. Squeeze the vinegar out of the steel wool and wrap it around the thermometer from cup B. Cover both cups with plastic wrap. Record the temperature every 2 minutes for 10 minutes. **Observe** what happens to the steel wool.

Time (minutes)	Temperature (°C)	
	Cup A	**Cup B**
Start		
2		
4		
6		
8		
10		

Explain Your Results

1. Observe: What happened to the temperature in cup A and cup B?

_____

_____

2. Interpret Data: Which cup had a chemical change? How can you tell?

_____

_____

Self-Assessment Checklist

I followed instructions to set up cups A and B and record the temperatures.   _____

I followed instructions to soak one piece of steel wool in vinegar for 1 minute.   _____

I followed instructions to wrap both thermometers with steel wool and recorded the temperatures every 2 minutes for 10 minutes.   _____

I described what happened to the temperature in cup A and cup B.   _____

I **interpreted my data** to name which cup had a chemical change and how I could tell.   _____

Notes for Home: Your child did an activity to **observe** a replacement reaction.
Home Activity: With your child, think of other examples of chemical changes.

Activity Book

Explore: How can you learn about the motion of a pendulum?

2 Pull back the pendulum 30 cm. Let go. **Observe** how the speed changes during a swing. Where does the washer move fastest? slowest? Where does it speed up? slow down?

_____

_____

_____

3 Test again from 30 cm back. Time 5 swings.
_____ seconds

4 **Predict** how pulling back the pendulum 60 cm would affect the time needed for 5 swings.

_____

Test your prediction. Time 5 swings.
1. _____ seconds

Explain Your Results

1. Compare the time needed for 30 cm and 60 cm swings. **Infer** how the distance a pendulum swings affects the time a swing takes.

_____

_____

2. Predict: Suppose the string was shortened. How do you think this would affect the time a swing takes? Explain.

_____

_____

Self-Assessment Checklist	
I followed instructions to make and **observe** a pendulum.	_____
I timed 5 short swings and **predicted** the time needed for a long swing.	_____
I compared my **prediction** to my results.	_____
I made an **inference** about how the distance a pendulum swings affects the time a swing takes.	_____
I **predicted** how shortening the string would affect the time a swing takes. I explained the reasoning that led to my prediction.	_____

Notes for Home: Your child did an activity to **observe** the motion of a pendulum.
Home Activity: With your child, **predict** whether mass affects the time it takes for a pendulum to swing.

154 Directed Inquiry

Activity Book

© Pearson Education, Inc.

Investigate: How can you describe motion?

3 Design and construct a data table.

4 Graph the distance the ball travels and the time it takes.

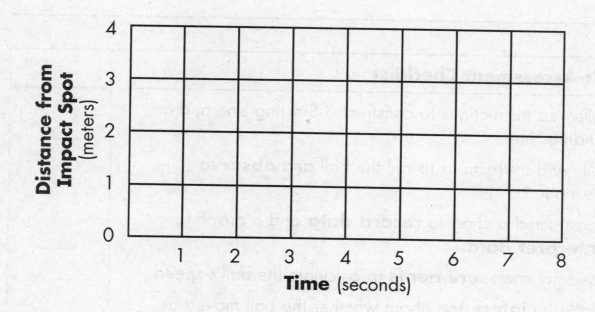

Distance from Impact Spot (meters)

Time (seconds)

Explain Your Results

1. Using your **measurements,** find the ball's speed from the Starting
Line to the Impact Spot. Find the speed from the Impact Spot to the
Ending Line. (speed = distance ÷ time)

_____

_____

2. Infer: Did the ball move at a steady speed? Explain your answer.

_____

_____

Go Further

How would your graph be different if you showed your results in feet
instead of meters? Find out. Write a report of your results in your science
journal.

_____

Self-Assessment Checklist	
I followed instructions to construct a Starting Line and an Ending Line.	_____
I followed instructions to roll the ball and **observe** its motion.	_____
I constructed a chart to **record data** and a graph to **interpret data.**	_____
I used my **measurements** to calculate the ball's speed.	_____
I made an **inference** about whether the ball moved at a steady speed. I explained the reasoning that led to my inference.	_____

Notes for Home: Your child did an activity to **observe** and **measure** the direction,
distance, and speed of a moving object.
Home Activity: With your child, discuss factors that affect the speed of a moving
object.

Lab zone Activity

How does inertia affect motion?

Materials

5 wooden blocks

ruler

What to Do

1 Stack the blocks on top of each other on a desktop.

2 Using the ruler, lightly tap the block on the bottom of the stack several times in a row. **Observe** what happens to the rest of the blocks.

3 Restack the blocks. Use the ruler to hit the bottom block quickly and with force. **Observe** what happens to the rest of the blocks.

4 Restack the blocks. Lightly tap the middle block with the ruler several times in a row. **Observe** what happens to the rest of the blocks.

5 Restack the blocks. Use the ruler to hit the middle block quickly and with force. **Observe** what happens to the rest of the blocks.

Explain Your Results

1. **Observe** What differences occurred when you hit the blocks with force compared to when you lightly tapped the blocks? Why did this happen?

2. **Infer** If you wanted to remove the bottom book from a stack of books without moving any of the other books, what would be the best way to do this?

Process Skills

You can make an **inference** based on your **observations** about inertia in this activity.

25

Use with Chapter 13

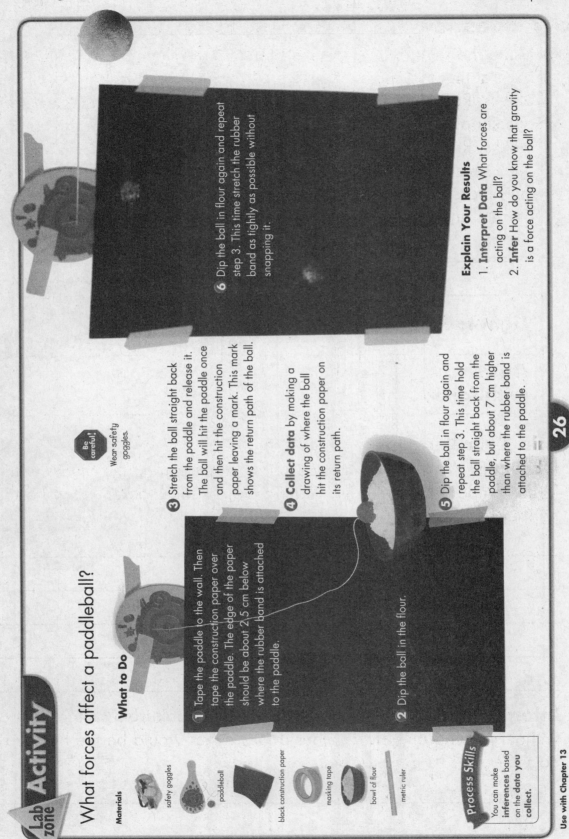

Activity

What forces affect a paddleball?

Materials

safety goggles

paddleball

black construction paper

masking tape

bowl of flour

metric ruler

Be careful!
Wear safety goggles.

What to Do

1 Tape the paddle to the wall. Then tape the construction paper over the paddle. The edge of the paper should be about 2.5 cm below where the rubber band is attached to the paddle.

2 Dip the ball in the flour.

3 Stretch the ball straight back from the paddle and release it. The ball will hit the paddle once and then hit the construction paper leaving a mark. This mark shows the return path of the ball.

4 **Collect data** by making a drawing of where the ball hit the construction paper on its return path.

5 Dip the ball in flour again and repeat step 3. This time hold the ball straight back from the paddle, but about 7 cm higher than where the rubber band is attached to the paddle.

6 Dip the ball in flour again and repeat step 3. This time stretch the rubber band as tightly as possible without snapping it.

Explain Your Results

1. **Interpret Data** What forces are acting on the ball?

2. **Infer** How do you know that gravity is a force acting on the ball?

Process Skills

You can make **inferences** based on the **data** you collect.

How does inertia affect motion?

2-**5** Using the ruler, lightly tap the block on the bottom of the stack several times in a row. **Observe** what happens to the rest of the blocks. Restack the blocks. Use the ruler to hit the bottom block quickly and with force. **Observe** what happens to the rest of the blocks. Restack the blocks. Lightly tap the middle block with the ruler several times in a row. **Observe** what happens to the rest of the blocks. Restack the blocks. Use the ruler to hit the middle block quickly and with force. **Observe** what happens to the rest of the blocks.

	Bottom block	**Middle block**
Light tap		
Quick tap with force		

Explain Your Results

1. Observe: What differences occurred when you hit the blocks with force compared to when you lightly tapped the blocks? Why did this happen?

_____

_____

_____

_____

_____

2. Infer: If you wanted to remove the bottom book from a stack of books without moving any of the other books, what would be the best way to do this?

_____

Self-Assessment Checklist	
I lightly tapped the block on the bottom and **observed** the rest of the blocks.	_____
I hit the bottom block quickly and with force and **observed** the rest of the blocks.	_____
I lightly tapped the middle block and **observed** the rest of the blocks.	_____
I hit the middle block quickly and with force and **observed** the rest of the blocks.	_____
I made an **inference** about the best way to remove the bottom book from a stack.	_____

Notes for Home: Your child did an activity to **observe** how inertia affects motion.
Home Activity: With your child, discuss why it's easier to make a ball roll on a smooth surface.

What forces affect a paddleball?

3–6 Collect data by making a drawing of where the ball hit the construction paper on its return path. Repeat step 3 but hold the ball 7 cm higher than where the rubber band is attached to the paddle. Repeat step 3 again and this time stretch the rubber band as tightly as possible without snapping it.

Explain Your Results

1. Interpret Data: What forces are acting on the ball?

_____

2. Infer: How do you know that gravity is a force acting on the ball?

_____

_____

Self-Assessment Checklist

I stretched the ball straight back and **collected data** about where it hit the paper.   _____

I held the ball 7 cm higher than where the rubber band was attached to the paddle.   _____

I stretched the rubber band as tight as possible without snapping it.   _____

I **interpreted my data** to explain what forces were acting on the ball.   _____

I made an **inference** about how I know gravity is a force acting on the ball.   _____

Notes for Home: Your child did an activity to examine the effect of gravity.
Home Activity: With your child, think of another way to counteract the force of gravity and keep a ball from falling right away.

Activity Book

© Pearson Education, Inc.

Explore: How can energy change its form?

1 Fill a jar $\frac{1}{2}$ full with sand. Put a thermometer in the jar. After 1 minute, record the temperature.

_____

2–3 Put on the lid. Take turns shaking the jar as hard as possible for a total of 10 minutes. **Measure** the temperature of the sand again and record it.

_____

Explain Your Results

Infer: Was thermal energy produced? How do you know? What was the source of this energy?

_____

_____

_____

Self-Assessment Checklist	
I followed instructions to fill a jar $\frac{1}{2}$ full with sand.	_____
I put a thermometer in the jar and recorded the temperature after 1 minute.	_____
I shook the jar as hard as possible for 10 minutes.	_____
I **measured** the temperature of the sand again and recorded it.	_____
I made **inferences** about whether thermal energy was produced and what the source was.	_____

Notes for Home: Your child did an activity to explore how energy can change forms.
Home Activity: With your child, discuss 2 appliances that convert electrical energy to heat energy.

Investigate: How does light move?

④ Collect Data: Show the processes you observe. Copy the diagram in your textbook or select a way of your own. Write these words on the correct lines: *reflection*, *refraction*, and *transmission* (going through).

Explain Your Results

1. What happens to the light that shines on the foil?

_____

2. Interpret Data: What happens to the direction of the light when it moves from air to water?

_____

3. What colors of light shine into the blue water? What color shines onto the paper? What color passes through the blue water (transmission)? What colors does the blue water block or filter out (absorption)?

_____

_____

Go Further

Use your equipment to investigate how shadows are formed. What conditions are needed? What objects cast dark shadows? Can a clear object cast a shadow? Make a plan to find out. Write clear instructions that others could follow.

_____

_____

_____

_____

_____

Self-Assessment Checklist	
I followed instructions to set up the cup and **observed** the light from above.	_____
I **collected data** for the processes I observed.	_____
I described what happens to the light that shines on the foil.	_____
I **interpreted my data** to explain what happens to the light when it moves from air to water.	_____
I explained how the different processes affected the color of the light.	_____

Notes for Home: Your child did an activity about the movement of light.
Home Activity: With your child, discuss how a rainbow is formed.

© Pearson Education, Inc.

Lab zone Activity

How do waves move?

Materials

large metal or plastic spring

What to Do

1 With a partner, stretch the spring out along a smooth surface. The distance between the coils should be about 1 cm.

2 Have one person start a wave through the spring by moving the spring quickly to the side and then back to the original starting place. **Observe** the motion of the wave as it moves down the spring. Repeat this action several times.

3 Have one person reach out in front and pull a few coils back. Then quickly let go of the pinched coils. **Observe** the motion of the wave as it moves down the spring. Repeat this several times.

4 Have your partner start a sideways wave. At the same time, you start a sideways wave in the same direction as your partner. **Observe** what happens when the two waves meet and pass through each other.

5 Have your partner start a sideways wave. At the same time, you start a sideways wave in the opposite direction as your partner. **Observe** what happens when the two waves meet and pass through each other.

Explain Your Results

1. **Collect Data** Make a chart to organize your observations. Identify the type of wave produced in each of the steps. Include drawings of the waves when possible.

2. **Interpret Data** How can you explain the differences in wave behavior when comparing the outcome of step 4 with the outcome of step 5?

Process Skills

Organizing the **data** you **collect** into a table or chart can help you analyze your results.

Lab zone Activity

What happens when you mix colors?

Materials

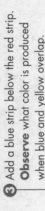

red, blue, and yellow
transparent plastic sheets

ruler

scissors

white paper

What to Do

1. Use the scissors and the ruler to cut the plastic sheets into strips, about 5 cm wide.

Be careful! Use care when handling sharp objects.

2. Place a red strip and a yellow strip perpendicular to each other along two edges of the white paper. The corner of the two strips should overlap and produce an orange color.

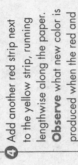

3. Add a blue strip below the red strip. **Observe** what color is produced when blue and yellow overlap.

4. Add another red strip next to the yellow strip, running lengthwise along the paper. **Observe** what new color is produced when the red and blue overlap.

5. Continue to add strips to fill the rest of the paper. Make sure there is at least one part where all of the strips overlap.

Explain Your Results

1. **Collect Data** Draw the grid and label the new colors produced. Include what colors are overlapping to make the new colors.

2. **Infer** How is the color black formed?

Process Skills

Collecting data can involve making drawings or writing descriptions of results.

© Pearson Education, Inc.

28

How do waves move?

Explain Your Results

1. Collecting Data: Make a chart to organize your observations. Identify the type of wave produced in each of the steps. Include drawings of the waves when possible.

2. Interpreting Data: How can you explain the differences in wave behavior when comparing the outcome of step 4 with the outcome of step 5?

_____

_____

_____

_____

Self-Assessment Checklist	
I followed instructions to stretch the spring out along a smooth surface.	_____
I **observed** the different kinds of waves that I created.	_____
I made a chart in which to **collect data.**	_____
I identified the type of wave produced in each step and made drawings of the waves.	_____
I **interpreted my data** to explain the differences in wave behavior in step 4 and step 5.	_____

Notes for Home: Your child did an activity to **observe** how waves move.
Home Activity: With your child, name 3 forms in which waves can appear (such as sound).

What happens when you mix colors?

Explain Your Results

1. Collect Data: Draw the grid and label the new colors produced.
Include what colors are overlapping to make the new colors.

2. Infer: How is the color black formed?

_____

Self-Assessment Checklist	
I followed instructions to cut the plastic and place the red and yellow strips on the paper.	_____
I added a blue strip and then a red strip and **observed** the new colors that were produced.	_____
I filled the rest of the paper with the strips, making sure they all overlapped in one part.	_____
I **collected data** by drawing a grid and labeling the colors produced.	_____
I made an **inference** about how the color black is formed.	_____

Notes for Home: Your child did an activity to **observe** what happens when you mix colors.
Home Activity: With your child, discuss why white is not the color formed in the spot where all the colors overlap.

Explore: What can electricity flow through?

❷ Predict which objects electricity will flow through. Test each object.
Observe. Does the bulb light up?

_____

_____

_____

Explain Your Results

1. Were your **predictions** correct? How do you know?

_____

_____

_____

2. How are the objects that electricity flows through alike?

_____

Self-Assessment Checklist	
I followed instructions to connect the wires, battery, and bulb.	_____
I **predicted** which objects electricity would flow through.	_____
I held the wire and the bulb against each object and **observed** if the bulb lit up.	_____
I explained whether or not my **predictions** were correct. I explained that the bulb lighted when electricity flowed through an object.	_____
I described how the objects that electricity flowed through were alike.	_____

Notes for Home: Your child did an activity to make a simple circuit and test whether objects conducted electricity.
Home Activity: With your child, discuss what materials a wire is made of and why.

Investigate: How are series and parallel circuits different?

①–④ First make a series circuit. Connect all the parts in each circuit. Record what happens to the light bulbs in each circuit in the chart. Unscrew a light bulb from the series circuit and a light bulb from the parallel circuit. Record what happens. Repeat with a parallel circuit. Draw a sketch or diagram of both circuits.

Circuit	Diagram of Circuit	Observations
Series Circuit		
Parallel Circuit		

Explain Your Results

1. Interpret Data: What is the difference between a series circuit and a parallel circuit? Use your diagrams to help describe the circuits and explain your ideas.

_____

_____

_____

2. Communicate: What paths can electricity take through a series circuit and a parallel circuit? Draw arrows on your diagrams to help explain how the electricity moves through the circuits.

_____

_____

_____

_____

Go Further

Construct a circuit of your own design using available resources. Select and use the appropriate tools. Diagram, test, and evaluate your circuit. Tell what limited your design. Describe your circuit and what you learned to other students.

_____

_____

_____

Self-Assessment Checklist	
I made a series circuit and recorded what happened when a light bulb was removed.	_____
I made a parallel circuit and recorded what happened when a light bulb was removed.	_____
I drew a sketch or a diagram of each circuit.	_____
I **interpreted my data** and explained the difference between the types of circuits.	_____
I **communicated** what paths electricity can take through the circuits with arrows on my diagrams.	_____

 Notes for Home: Your child did an activity to compare a series and a parallel circuit.
Home Activity: With your child, discuss why a parallel circuit might be used instead of a series circuit and vice-versa.

© Pearson Education, Inc.

Lab zone Activity

How can you use insulators and conductors to make a game?

Materials

thick cardboard and aluminum foil

tape

battery

light bulb

bolt

nail

3 pieces of insulated copper wire

What to Do

1 Wrap the cardboard with aluminum foil and tape the foil to the back of the cardboard.

2 Plan out your game. Draw a path that could be tricky to follow on the aluminum foil.

3 Cover the path you drew with tape.

4 Use the nail to make a hole in one corner through the aluminum foil and the cardboard. Attach the wires as shown.

How can you make your game more difficult?

Process Skills

Interpreting data helps you draw a conclusion about the results of an experiment.

5 Trade games with your partner.

6 Play the game. The object of the game is to trace the tape path with the bolt without touching the aluminum. You lose the game when the light bulb turns on.

Explain Your Results

1. **Interpret Data** How do you know that the foil is a conductor? How do you know that the tape is an insulator?

2. **Infer** How does an insulator work?

29

Activity

Lab Zone

How can you map a magnet's magnetic field?

Materials

large sheet of paper

bar magnet

compass

pencil

What to Do

1. Spread the sheet of paper out on a desk or table. Place the bar magnet in the middle of the paper.

2. Place the compass about 2.5 cm from the bottom end of the magnet and wait for the needle to settle. Make a mark on the paper to show the direction the needle is pointing.

3. Move the compass up about 1 cm toward the top of the magnet. Wait for the needle to settle and mark its direction on the paper.

4. Repeat step 3, moving the compass toward the top of the magnet and coming down around the other side back to the bottom. When you finish, you will have a pattern that shows the magnetic field around the magnet.

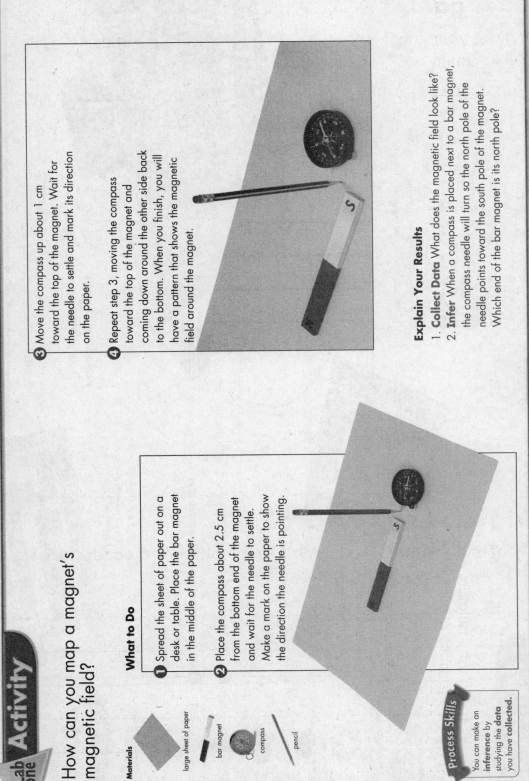

Process Skills

You can make an **inference** by studying the **data** you have **collected**.

Explain Your Results

1. **Collect Data** What does the magnetic field look like?

2. **Infer** When a compass is placed next to a bar magnet, the compass needle will turn so the north pole of the needle points toward the south pole of the magnet. Which end of the bar magnet is its north pole?

30

Activity Book

How can you use insulators and conductors to make a game?

2 Plan out your game. Draw a path that could be difficult to follow on the aluminum foil.

Explain Your Results

1. Interpret Data: How do you know that foil is a conductor? How do you know that the tape is an insulator?

_____

_____

_____

_____

_____

2. Infer: How does an insulator work?

_____

Self-Assessment Checklist

I followed instructions to draw a game and outline the path using foil strips.	_____
I followed instructions to attach the wires to the cardboard, battery, and light bulb holder.	_____
I traced the path of my partner's game.	_____
I **interpreted my data** to explain how to tell that foil is a conductor and tape is an insulator.	_____
I made an **inference** about how an insulator works.	_____

Notes for Home: Your child did an activity to explore how insulators and conductors work.
Home Activity: With your child, name 2 more insulators and 2 more conductors.

How can you map a magnet's magnetic field?

Explain Your Results

1. Collect Data: What does the magnetic field look like?

_____

_____

2. Infer: When a compass is placed next to a bar magnet, the compass needle will turn so the north pole of the needle points toward the south pole of the magnet. Which end of the bar magnet is the north pole?

_____

_____

_____

Self-Assessment Checklist	
I followed instructions to spread out the sheet of paper and place the magnet in the middle.	
I followed instructions to move the compass around the magnet.	_____
I marked on the sheet of paper where the needle was pointing during the different steps.	_____
I **collected data** about what the magnetic field looked like.	_____
I made an **inference** about which end of the bar magnet is the north pole.	_____

© Pearson Education, Inc.

Notes for Home: Your child did an activity to map a magnet's magnetic field.
Home Activity: With your child, discuss why magnets attract or repel each other.

Name _____

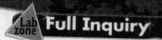
Experiment: Can you change the poles of an electromagnet?

Ask a question.

Does the direction in which electric current flows through an electromagnet affect the locations of its poles?

State a hypothesis.

_____

_____

_____

Identify and control variables.

You will change the direction in which the electrons move through an electromagnet. You will observe the locations of the poles on an electromagnet before and after you change the direction the electrons move. Everything else must stay the same, including the number of coils on the electromagnet. Identify the **variables.**

Independent variable _____

Dependent variable _____

Controlled variables _____

_____

Test your hypothesis.

❶–❺ Follow the steps to complete your experiment.

Collect and record your data.

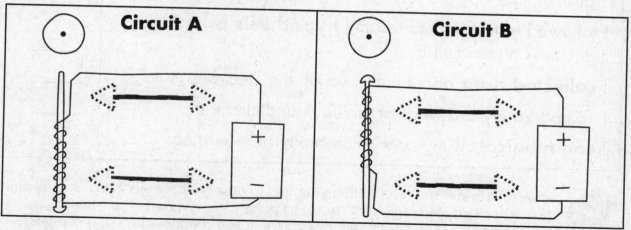

© Pearson Education, Inc.

Interpret your data.

Analyze the drawings that show your data for the **experiment.** What direction are the electrons moving in each circuit? Where is the north pole located in each drawing?

_____

_____

State your conclusion.

Explain how reversing the direction the electrons move through an electromagnet affects the locations of its poles. Compare your hypothesis with your results. **Communicate** your conclusion orally or in writing.

_____

_____

_____

Go Further

How do the poles of 2 electromagnets affect each other? Work with another group to develop a plan to find out.

_____

_____

Self-Assessment Checklist	
I stated my **hypothesis** about the effect of the direction of the current on the location of the poles.	_____
I followed instructions to test my **hypothesis** by making circuit A and circuit B.	_____
I **collected data** about the direction the electrons moved.	_____
I compared my drawings of circuit A and circuit B.	_____
I **communicated** my conclusion orally or in writing.	_____

Notes for Home: Your child did an activity to **observe** how reversing the direction of current in an electromagnet causes its poles to be reversed.
Home Activity: With your child, discuss the role a magnet plays in a compass.

Explore: How can you make an astrolabe?

Record the angle of the paper star in your classroom.

_____ degrees

Explain Your Results
Communicate: How does an astrolabe measure the angle of a star?

_____

_____

Why did different students get different angles for the paper star?

_____

_____

Self-Assessment Checklist	
I followed instructions to glue the Astrolabe Pattern onto cardboard.	
I followed instructions to cut out the astrolabe and tape it onto a straw.	_____
I looked at the paper star and determined the angle where the string crosses the numbered scale.	_____
I tried to locate stars, constellations, and planets.	_____
I **communicated** why different students got different readings for the location of the paper star.	_____

Notes for Home: Your child did an activity to make an astrolabe.
Home Activity: With your child, discuss why astronomers study the location of stars.

Name ______________________

Lab zone **Guided Inquiry**

Use with Chapter 16, pp. 530–531

Investigate: What does a spiral galaxy look like from different angles?

2 **Observe** the cups from directly above the table. This view represents the galaxy as seen from outside the galaxy. Draw a sketch or diagram of what you see in the chart below.

3–4 Kneel beside the cups on the edge of the table. Look across the table at the other side of the cups. This view represents the galaxy as seen from a planet near the galaxy's edge. Draw a diagram of what you see.

Model of a Spiral Galaxy	
View from Above	**View from the Edge**

Explain Your Results

1. How did the angle from which you view your **model** affect what you saw?

____

____

____

2. How is the model like a spiral galaxy? How is it different?

____

____

____

3. Predict. Suppose you made a model of an elliptical galaxy. When seen from above, would it look the same as a spiral galaxy? When seen from the edge, would it look the same as a spiral galaxy? Test your prediction.

_____

_____

_____

Go Further

If possible in your area, observe stars in the night sky. Use a sky chart to help find our galaxy, the Milky Way. Also try to identify stars in the night sky that are unusually bright or ones that appear slightly red or blue.

_____

_____

_____

Self-Assessment Checklist	
I **observed** the cups from above the table the edge of the table and drew a sketch of what I saw.	_____
I described how angles from which I viewed my **model** affected what I saw.	_____
I determined how the **model** is like a spiral galaxy and how it is different.	_____
I **predicted** what a **model** of an elliptical galaxy would look like when seen from above and when seen from the galaxy's edge.	_____
I tested predictions about a model of an elliptical galaxy.	_____

Notes for Home: Your child did an activity to make and **observe** a **model** of a spiral galaxy.
Home Activity: Have your child explain to you what the solar system is.

Lab zone Activity

What happens as the universe expands?

Materials

balloon

markers

metric ruler

What to Do

1. Use the red marker to draw one dot on an empty balloon.

2. Use the black marker to draw four dots on the balloon. Place each black dot a different distance from the red dot.

3. Measure the distance from each black dot to the red dot. Record the distances.

4. Blow up the balloon part way. Hold it closed with your fingers.

5. Have your partner measure and record the distances between the dots.

6. Finish blowing up the balloon, making a knot to hold it closed. Repeat step 5.

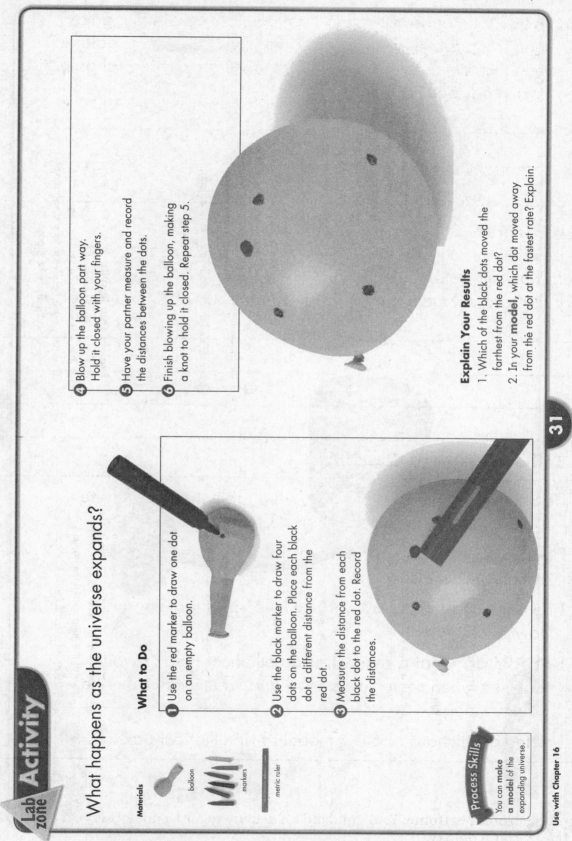

Explain Your Results

1. Which of the black dots moved the farthest from the red dot?

2. In your **model**, which dot moved away from the red dot at the fastest rate? Explain.

Process Skills

You can make **a model** of the expanding universe.

31

Lab zone Activity

What happens during an eclipse?

Materials

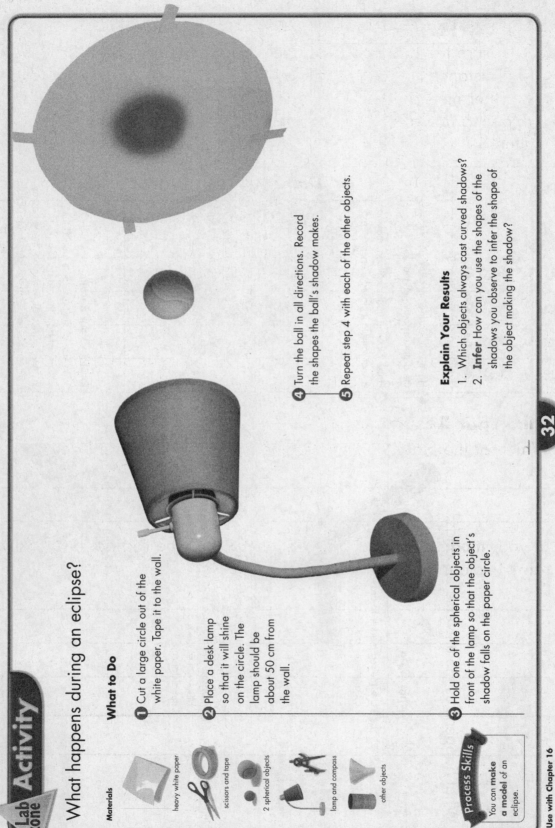

heavy white paper

scissors and tape

2 spherical objects

lamp and compass

other objects

What to Do

1. Cut a large circle out of the white paper. Tape it to the wall.

2. Place a desk lamp so that it will shine on the circle. The lamp should be about 50 cm from the wall.

3. Hold one of the spherical objects in front of the lamp so that the object's shadow falls on the paper circle.

4. Turn the ball in all directions. Record the shapes the ball's shadow makes.

5. Repeat step 4 with each of the other objects.

Explain Your Results

1. Which objects always cast curved shadows?

2. **Infer** How can you use the shapes of the shadows you observe to infer the shape of the object making the shadow?

Process Skills

You can **make a model** of an eclipse.

32

Activity Book

What happens as the universe expands?

③—⑥ Measure the distance from each black dot to the red dot. Record the distances in the chart. Blow up the balloon part way. Have your partner measure and record the distances between the dots. Finish blowing up the balloon, making a knot to hold it closed. Repeat step 5.

	Distance to Red Dot (cm)		
	Empty Balloon	**Partially Full Balloon**	**Full Balloon**
Black Dot 1			
Black Dot 2			
Black Dot 3			
Black Dot 4			

Explain Your Results

1. Which of the black dots moved the farthest from the red dot?

_____

_____

2. In your **model,** which dot moved away from the red dot at the fastest rate? Explain.

_____

_____

_____

_____

_____

Self-Assessment Checklist	
I followed instructions to draw a red dot and black dots on an empty balloon.	_____
I measured and recorded the distance from each black dot to the red dot.	_____
I measured and recorded the distances between the dots at each step.	_____
I named the numbered dot that moved the farthest from the red dot.	_____
I concluded which dot moved away from the red dot at the fastest rate in my **model** and explained my answer.	

Notes for Home: Your child did an activity to **make a model** of the expanding universe.
Home Activity: With your child, find a recent article in the science section of your newspaper about current research on the universe.

Activity Book

What happens during an eclipse?

4–**5** Turn the ball in all directions. Record the shapes the ball's shadow makes. Repeat step 4 with each of the objects.

Object	Shapes Made by Shadow

Explain Your Results

1. Which objects always cast curved shadows?

_____

_____

2. Infer: How can you use the shapes of the shadows you observe to infer the shape of the object making the shadow?

_____

_____

Self-Assessment Checklist	
I followed instructions to cut out a large sheet of white paper and tape it to the wall.	_____
I followed instructions to place a desk lamp so that it would shine on the circle.	_____
I held each object in front of the lamp and recorded the shape of the shadow it made.	_____
I described which objects always cast curved shadows.	_____
I explained how I could use the shapes of the shadows to **infer** the shapes of the objects.	_____

Notes for Home: Your child did an activity to **make a model** of an eclipse.
Home Activity: With your child, research when the next eclipse will be in your area.

Explore: Does distance affect orbiting time?

Explain Your Results

1. Which ball hit the ground first?

_____

2. Infer: Think about your answer. How might a planet's distance from the Sun affect the time needed to make one orbit?

_____

_____

Self-Assessment Checklist	
I followed instructions to make 2 clay balls and push them onto a meterstick and a ruler.	_____
I let go of the meterstick and the ruler at the same time.	_____
I **observed** what happened.	_____
I described which ball hit the ground first.	_____
I made an **inference** about how distance from the Sun affects orbiting time.	_____

Notes for Home: Your child did an activity to determine whether a planet's distance from the Sun affects the time it takes to orbit the Sun.
Home Activity: With your child, discuss how life on Earth would be different if its orbit was twice as long.

Investigate: Why do we see the phases of the Moon?

5 Look through each hole. Record your **observations.**

Phases of the Moon		
Hole	**Drawing of Moon Phase**	**Name of Moon Phase** (Description)
A		
B		
C		
D		

Explain Your Results

1. In your **model,** your flashlight always lights half of the "moon." Why does the "moon" appear to be completely lighted when viewed through one hole?

_____

_____

2. Why does the "moon" not appear to be lighted when viewed through one hole?

_____

_____

_____

Go Further

How could you change your model to show a crescent Moon? Develop
a plan to answer this or any other question you may have.

_____

_____

_____

_____

Self-Assessment Checklist	
I followed instructions to **make a model.**	_____
I looked through each hole and recorded my **observations.**	_____
I determined why the "moon" appears to be completely lighted when viewed through one hole.	_____
I determined why the "moon" does not appear to be lighted when viewed through one hole.	_____

Notes for Home: Your child did an activity to investigate why we see the phases of the Moon.
Home Activity: With your child, observe the Moon and identify which phase it is.

© Pearson Education, Inc.

Name _____

Lab zone Activity

How can you model day and night?

Materials

skewer and 2 plastic drinking straws

ball

marker

scissors and glue

poster board and compass

sticker

lamp

What to Do

1. Push the skewer through the center of the ball. You have made a **model** of Earth on its axis.

   Be careful! Be careful with the sharp end of the skewer.

2. Hold the ball so that the skewer points straight up and down. Use a marker to draw a line around the center of the ball. This is Earth's equator.

3. Use the scissors to cut two pieces of straw. Each piece should be as long as the part of the skewer that sticks out of the ball. Put a piece of straw over each end of the skewer.

4. Use the compass to draw a circle on each piece of poster board. Cut out the circles.

   The circle should be 5 cm wider than the ball.

5. Cover the inside of each piece of poster board with glue. Place your Earth model between the two layers of poster board. Make sure your Earth is titled on its axis. Place a sticker on the ball to represent the part of Earth on which you live.

   Midnight

6. Shine the lamp on Earth's equator. Spin Earth counterclockwise. **Observe** what happens to the part of Earth where the sticker is placed.

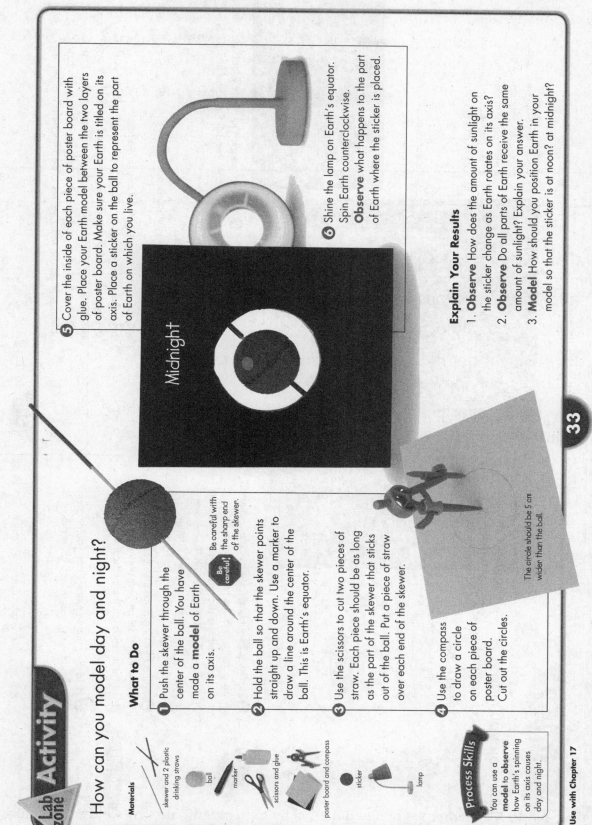

Explain Your Results

1. **Observe** How does the amount of sunlight on the sticker change as Earth rotates on its axis?

2. **Observe** Do all parts of Earth receive the same amount of sunlight? Explain your answer.

3. **Model** How should you position Earth in your model so that the sticker is at noon? at midnight?

Process Skills

You can use a **model** to **observe** how Earth's spinning on its axis causes day and night.

33

Activity

How can you map a landscape you cannot see?

Materials

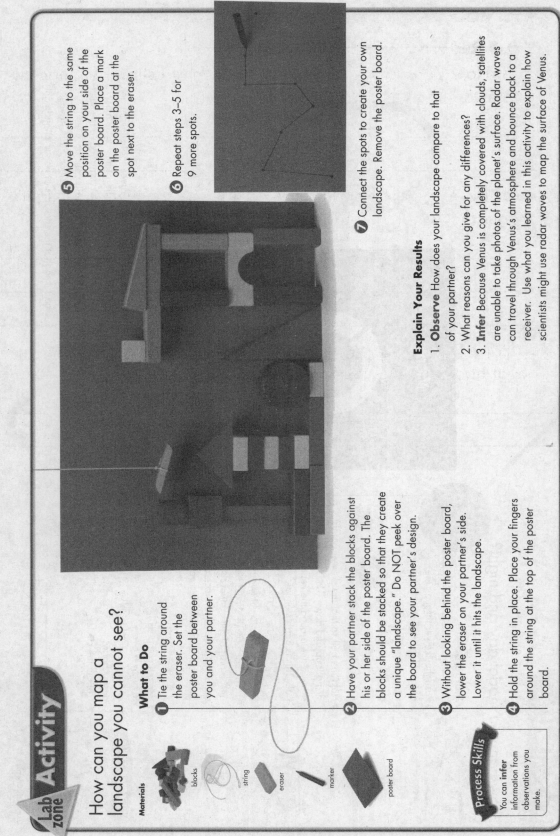

blocks

string

eraser

marker

poster board

What to Do

1. Tie the string around the eraser. Set the poster board between you and your partner.

2. Have your partner stack the blocks against his or her side of the poster board. The blocks should be stacked so that they create a unique "landscape." Do NOT peek over the board to see your partner's design.

3. Without looking behind the poster board, lower the eraser on your partner's side. Lower it until it hits the landscape.

4. Hold the string in place. Place your fingers around the string at the top of the poster board.

5. Move the string to the same position on your side of the poster board. Place a mark on the poster board at the spot next to the eraser.

6. Repeat steps 3–5 for 9 more spots.

7. Connect the spots to create your own landscape. Remove the poster board.

Explain Your Results

1. **Observe** How does your landscape compare to that of your partner?

2. What reasons can you give for any differences?

3. **Infer** Because Venus is completely covered with clouds, satellites are unable to take photos of the planet's surface. Radar waves can travel through Venus's atmosphere and bounce back to a receiver. Use what you learned in this activity to explain how scientists might use radar waves to map the surface of Venus.

Process Skills

You can **infer** information from observations you make.

How can you model day and night?

Explain Your Results

1. Observe: How does the amount of sunlight on the sticker change as Earth rotates on its axis?

_____

_____

2. Observe: Do all parts of Earth receive the same amount of sunlight? Explain your answer.

_____

_____

_____

3. Model: How should you position Earth in your model so that the sticker is at noon? at midnight?

_____

_____

Self-Assessment Checklist	
I followed instructions to **make a model** of Earth on its axis.	_____
I followed instructions to place the Earth model between two layers of posterboard.	_____
I **observed** how the amount of sunlight on the sticker changes as the Earth rotates on its axis.	_____
I **observed** whether all parts of Earth receive the same amount of sunlight.	_____
I described how I should position Earth in my **model** so that the sticker is at noon and midnight.	_____

 Notes for Home: Your child did an activity to **make a model** in order to **observe** how Earth's spinning on its axis causes day and night.
Home Activity: With your child, discuss how the position of the Earth is related to the seasons.

© Pearson Education, Inc.

How can you map a landscape you cannot see?

Explain Your Results

1. Observe: How does your landscape compare to that of your partner?

_____

_____

2. What reasons can you give for any differences?

_____

_____

3. Infer: Because Venus is completely covered with clouds, satellites are unable to take photos of the planet's surface. Radar waves can travel through Venus's atmosphere and bounce back to a receiver. Use what you learned in this activity to explain how scientists might use radar waves to map the surface of Venus.

_____

_____

_____

_____

_____

Self-Assessment Checklist	
I used the string with the eraser to examine my partner's landscape.	_____
I connected the spots to copy the landscape and removed the posterboard.	_____
I **observed** how my landscape compared to that of my partner.	_____
I gave reasons for the differences between the two landscapes.	_____
I explained how scientists might use radar waves to map the surface of Venus.	_____

Notes for Home: Your child did an activity to learn how scientists map a landscape they cannot see.
Home Activity: With your child, find information online or at your local library about what the surfaces of the different planets look like.

Explore: How can water be absorbed?

3 Turn the cup upside down on the table. **Observe.**

_____

_____

When you finish, **predict** how much more water the absorber can soak up—10 mL, 20 mL, or 30 mL. Design, write, and carry out a procedure to find out.

_____

_____

_____

_____

_____

Explain Your Results

1. For step 3, find the ratio of the volume of *water* to the volume of *absorber*.

$$\text{ratio} = \frac{\text{volume of water (mL)}}{\text{volume of absorber (mL)}}$$

_____

2. Based on your **observations** and experience, why do you think disposable diapers contain a water absorber?

_____

_____

_____

Self-Assessment Checklist	
I **measured** the water and poured it into the cup.	_____
I turned the cup upside down on the table and **observed** what happened.	_____
I made a **prediction** about how much more water the absorber could soak up.	_____
I calculated the ratio of the volume of the water to the volume of the absorber.	_____
I made an **inference** about why diapers might contain a water absorber like the one I tested.	_____

Notes for Home: Your child did an activity to **observe** what happens to water when it comes into contact with a water absorber.
Home Activity: With your child, **observe** two other household objects that absorb water and compare them to the water absorber studied in class.

Investigate: How do space probes send images to Earth?

5 **Compare** the images. Are they the same? Explain.

_____

_____

_____

Explain Your Results

1. How accurately was the signal received? Explain why it might not be perfectly accurate.

_____

_____

_____

_____

2. Based on the process you **modeled,** describe how an image is sent from a space probe.

_____

_____

_____

_____

_____

_____

3. Infer: How do you think cameras on satellites orbiting Earth send images back to Earth?

_____

_____

Go Further

What would happen if you "sent" to a partner a full-page picture drawn on a piece of graph paper with large squares and on a piece with small squares? Find out. Send both to a partner with matching graph paper. Does one take longer? Does one make a better picture? Explain.

_____

_____

_____

_____

Self-Assessment Checklist	
I followed instructions and worked with my partner to transfer the information on the Image Sending Grid to the Image Receiving Grid.	_____
I **compared** the two images and explained whether or not they were the same.	_____
I described how accurately the signal was received and explained why it might not be perfectly accurate.	
I described how an image is sent from a space probe, based on the process I **modeled**.	_____
I made an **inference** about how cameras on satellites orbiting Earth send images back to Earth.	_____

 Notes for Home: Your child did an activity about how space probes send images back to Earth.
Home Activity: With your child, **observe** some photographs taken by space probes.

© Pearson Education, Inc.

Name _____

© Pearson Education, Inc.

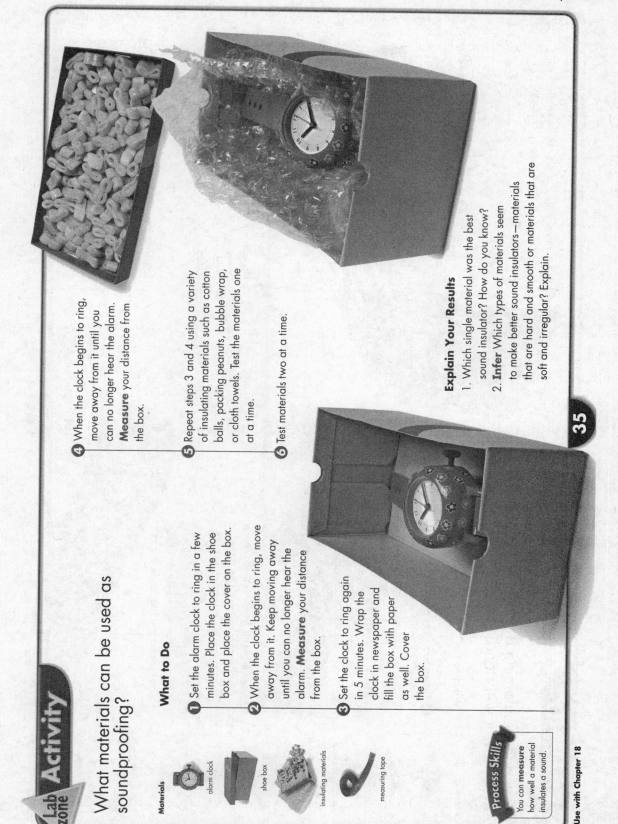

Lab zone Activity

What materials can be used as soundproofing?

Materials

alarm clock

shoe box

insulating materials

measuring tape

What to Do

1. Set the alarm clock to ring in a few minutes. Place the clock in the shoe box and place the cover on the box.

2. When the clock begins to ring, move away from it. Keep moving away until you can no longer hear the alarm. **Measure** your distance from the box.

3. Set the clock to ring again in 5 minutes. Wrap the clock in newspaper and fill the box with paper as well. Cover the box.

4. When the clock begins to ring, move away from it until you can no longer hear the alarm. **Measure** your distance from the box.

5. Repeat steps 3 and 4 using a variety of insulating materials such as cotton balls, packing peanuts, bubble wrap, or cloth towels. Test the materials one at a time.

6. Test materials two at a time.

Explain Your Results

1. Which single material was the best sound insulator? How do you know?

2. **Infer** Which types of materials seem to make better sound insulators—materials that are hard and smooth or materials that are soft and irregular? Explain.

Process Skills

You can **measure** how well a material insulates a sound.

35

Lab zone Activity

How does reinforcing a structure affect how it withstands force?

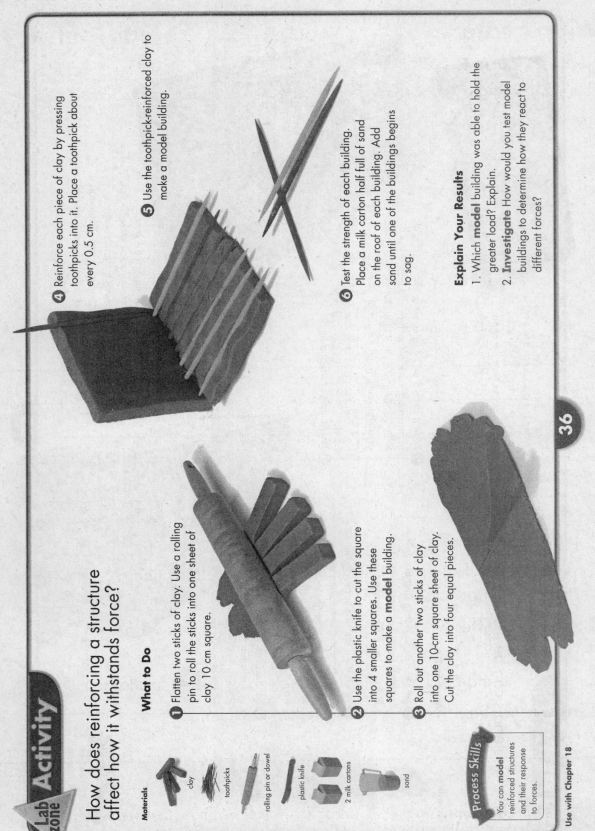

Materials

clay

toothpicks

rolling pin or dowel

plastic knife

2 milk cartons

sand

What to Do

1. Flatten two sticks of clay. Use a rolling pin to roll the sticks into one sheet of clay 10 cm square.

2. Use the plastic knife to cut the square into 4 smaller squares. Use these squares to make a **model** building.

3. Roll out another two sticks of clay into one 10-cm square sheet of clay. Cut the clay into four equal pieces.

4. Reinforce each piece of clay by pressing toothpicks into it. Place a toothpick about every 0.5 cm.

5. Use the toothpick-reinforced clay to make a model building.

6. Test the strength of each building. Place a milk carton half full of sand on the roof of each building. Add sand until one of the buildings begins to sag.

Explain Your Results

1. Which **model** building was able to hold the greater load? Explain.

2. **Investigate** How would you test model buildings to determine how they react to different forces?

Process Skills

You can model reinforced structures and their response to forces.

36

What materials can be used as soundproofing?

Explain Your Results

1. Which single material was the best sound insulator? How do you know?

_____

_____

_____

_____

2. Infer: Which types of materials seem to make better sound insulators—materials that are hard and smooth or materials that are soft and irregular? Explain.

_____

_____

_____

Self-Assessment Checklist	
I followed instructions to set the alarm clock to ring and to place it in the shoebox.	_____
I moved away from the clock when it began to ring until I could no longer hear it.	_____
I tested the different materials at first one and then two at a time.	_____
I named the material that was the single best sound insulator.	_____
I **inferred** about which types of materials seem to make better sound insulators.	_____

Notes for Home: Your child did an activity to examine how well different materials insulate sound.
Home Activity: With your child, find out what kinds of materials are used to make a room soundproof.

© Pearson Education, Inc.

How does reinforcing a structure affect how it withstands force?

Explain Your Results

1. Which **model** building was able to hold the greater load? Explain.

_____

_____

2. Investigate: How would you test model buildings to determine how they react to different forces?

_____

_____

_____

Self-Assessment Checklist	
I **made a model** of a building with the clay.	_____
I made another **model** of a building with the clay reinforced with toothpicks.	_____
I tested the strength of each building by placing a carton half full with sand on the roof.	_____
I explained which **model** building was able to hold the greater load.	_____
I described how to **investigate** model buildings to determine how they reacted to the forces.	_____

Notes for Home: Your child did an activity to **make a model** of a reinforced structure and its response to forces.
Home Activity: With your child, discuss other ways that buildings can be designed to withstand forces.

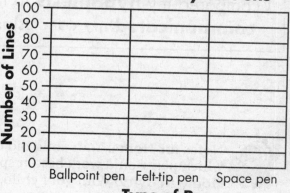
Experiment: Which writing tool might work best in space?

Ask a question.
How does gravity affect how well a pen writes?

State a hypothesis.
If you turn each pen upside down and make lines, then which pen will make the most lines? Write your **hypothesis.**

_____

Identify and control variables.
In this experiment, what is the independent variable? What is the dependent variable? What are some controlled variables?

Independent variable: _____

Dependent variable: _____

Controlled variables: _____

_____

Test your hypothesis.
Decide what you mean by a *line*. Make an **operational definition.**

_____

_____

_____

❶-❺ Follow the steps to perform your experiment. Record your data in the chart.

Collect and record your data.

Type of Pen	Number of Lines Use your operational definition.
Ballpoint pen	
Felt-tip pen	
Space pen	

Effect of Gravity on Pens

Number of Lines: 100, 90, 80, 70, 60, 50, 40, 30, 20, 10, 0

Type of Pen: Ballpoint pen, Felt-tip pen, Space pen

© Pearson Education, Inc.

Interpret your data.

Use your data to make a bar graph. Look at your graph closely. Which pens are most affected by gravity?

State your conclusion.

Describe your results. Compare your hypothesis with your results.
Communicate your conclusion.

_____

_____

Go Further

What would happen if you used a gel pen? Design and carry out a plan to investigate this or other questions you may have.

_____

_____

_____

Self-Assessment Checklist	
I stated my **hypothesis** about which pen would make the most lines if turned upside down.	_____
I **made an operational definition** of a line.	_____
I followed instructions to test my **hypothesis.**	_____
I **collected data** in a chart and **interpreted data** by making a bar graph.	_____
I compared my **hypothesis** to my results and **communicated** my conclusion.	_____

Notes for Home: Your child did an activity to make and test a **hypothesis** about which pen would work best in space.
Home Activity: With your child, discuss whether or not a mercury-filled thermometer would work in space.